T0380266

UNTRAMPLED SALT

MORE STORIES OF LOVE, MERCY, AND GRACE

DAVID G. BOWEN

WESTBOW
PRESS®
A DIVISION OF THOMAS NELSON
& ZONDERVAN

WestBow Press books may be ordered through booksellers or by contacting:

WestBow Press
A Division of Thomas Nelson & Zondervan
1663 Liberty Drive
Bloomington, IN 47403
www.westbowpress.com
844-714-3454

ISBN: 979-8-3850-2497-1 (sc)
ISBN: 979-8-3850-2498-8 (hc)
ISBN: 979-8-3850-2499-5 (e)

Library of Congress Control Number: 2024909028

Print information available on the last page.

WestBow Press rev. date: 06/25/2024

This book is dedicated to my helpmeet and wife, Billie Rose; to my precious children, John, Scott, and Melanie; and to my remarkable grandchildren, Kayla, Joshua, Noah, Reagan, and Hannah. Each of you is so loved!

CONTENTS

BRITISH CALEDONIAN AT FORTY-TWO THOUSAND FEET—A POEM

1

Don't you see that children are GOD's best gift?
—PSALM 127:3 (MSG)

Our wedding gift to each other was a king-size bed.

After we filed the "no fault" divorce papers on that Friday, I was left with the bed as a reminder of our now-failed marriage.

The good news was the children and I flew to England the following Monday to serve in a pastor exchange program for the summer.

I left the bed just as I was leaving that marriage.

One of my not-so-spiritual gifts is brooding and celebrating misery. I practiced that gift during the months we were in England.

Truth be, I was suffering and hurting. I decided to focus my energy on John and Lesley to make sure they were as well cared for as possible.

I made sure they were well fed. I ate as little as my subtly growing depression would allow me.

I made sure they had rest and sleep. I practiced staying awake for most of the nights.

One of the things on which I miserably brooded was what I was going to do when I returned home in late summer. How is a divorced person supposed to act? How is a divorced minister supposed to serve? Or should I begin planning to leave the ministry?

Time has a way of moving us to decisions we would rather not face.

At the end of summer, I sent John and Lesley home so they could begin the new school year. I would join them after a trip to my ancestral towns in Wales.

The British Caledonian jet was forty-two thousand feet over Greenland. I was going home divorced and looking at being a single parent, not in England fair but in that house.

It was over Canada that I decided to burn the bed. I would shoot it with my deer rifle, drag it into the woods behind the parsonage, and burn it.

Afterward, I slept on the hard floor, clutching myself around the shoulders, and crying all over except through my eyes.

Lesley Ayn, age five, came down the hall. Her footsteps paused at the door, waiting to know if the space inside was too painful to enter.

She quietly pushed open the door and walked to where I sat, a huddled mass straining to be me.

"Here," she said. "Take my bear. You cry better holding something."

BIBLE BARGAINS

> Every Scripture passage is inspired by God. All of them are
> useful for teaching, pointing out errors, correcting people,
> and training them for a life that has God's approval.
>
> —2 TIMOTHY 3:17 (GW)

Each generation of humans has a lot to say about the generation that follows. I remember hearing that going to college was sure to separate a student from their faith background.

I was thinking prayer would be a good example of a faith background. I learned in my first quarter that the day or two before midterm or final exams was a time of great praying all over the campus and in almost every dorm room.

I also learned that a great number of the prayers were actually bargaining. For instance, *If I can get a certain grade, then I promise to stop doing such and such* or *I promise to begin doing such and such.*

Elizabeth Kübler-Ross wrote that bargaining was one of the classic stages of grieving. Perhaps her outline of those stages need not be followed as if it is an immutable law. However, it is true that "coulda, shoulda, and woulda" make their way into many of our experiences of profound loss.

I was brought up with the memorization of one Bible verse as a way to move more quickly to eating supper. You might be surprised at the joy to be found in "Jesus wept" or the delight that you might find in "love one another." The verses get longer and more difficult after those two.

The kinship of bargaining and Bible verses were again brought to reality for me in my seventeenth year of ministry as a pastor in a local congregation. I had set aside some time each week to spend in the church office in case someone wanted to drop by and talk about the things that church folks talk about with pastors. I did have that question about dogs going to heaven brought up in August 1994.

But the day I remember was the day Tim came by to talk. He wanted to get involved in a serious Bible study and wanted to start as soon as possible. He was a Vietnam veteran who had served in an infantry unit. Members of his unit were pulled aside on a regular basis to be "voluntold" to go on a long-range patrol (LRP) or a *lurp*. One late afternoon, Tim and the rest of his patrol were preparing for a mission to clandestinely move into enemy territory and set up a listening post to gather information about troop movements. A line in several movies came to mind as he shared his anxiety about that particular mission. It is a bargaining prayer with the Bible thrown in for good measure. "Lord, if I can return from this mission and then rotate home without serious wounds, I will begin at Genesis 1 and read your Word through to the end of Revelation."

I was honored to be in the presence of a combat veteran. I was impressed by his commitment to Bible study. I was a bit in awe at the depth of his prayer. I asked him, "How far did you get? In your Bible reading when you got home, how far did you get?"

He paused. "Second Chronicles."

Have you ever read 2 Chronicles? Having struggled with that book myself, I did not offer judgment or condemnation. I just gave him the information that he requested about the start of our next Bible study.

I DID AND I STILL DO

||||||||||||||||||||||||||||||||||||||||||||||||||||||||||||||||||||||||||||||||||||||||||||||||||||||||||||||||||||||||||||||||||||||||||||||

Then the LORD God said, "It is not good for the man to
be alone; I will make him a helper suitable for him."

—Genesis 2:18 (NASB)

I went through a lot of pain and hurt after my divorce, but some of that pain and hurt was taken away by the fact that I had full custody of my two precious children.

I dated some, but I was cautious. I had been a contributing part of a broken marriage. Four years after my divorce, I was attending a spiritual retreat.

There was some time to sit with a group of men who would listen to me, pray for me, and also pray with me.

My time to pray came. I opened my mouth and said, "God, please send a godly woman of your choosing into my life. Amen."

I believe that God likes to lovingly mess with men. He said to me as clearly as I type now, "Well, David, I gave you Billie Rose as a Christian friend two years ago. Did you think that was all I had in mind for you?"

Two years later, in 1989, we began to try to blend four children together as we married. However, since then, I have learned that I never officially, formally proposed marriage to Billie. Please, no hissing. She and I have talked, and as best we can, we have reconstructed some of what I apparently thought was my asking her to marry me.

We had been at the wedding rehearsal of friends. Afterward, we went to dinner and were discussing weddings in general. She recalls that I spoke the following: "We could do it during spring break. We could take the kids with us." Again, please no booing. Billie said that, later in the evening, she realized that I was talking about our getting married. Of course, I was.

So, right now, with you as my witnesses, I am in my office in the basement of our home and crawling around on one knee. I am practicing my lines. Let the record show that later this evening, February 13, 2024, I will ask Billie Rose to be my wife.

Now, for the rest of the story.

We were married at Wesley Chapel United Methodist Church near Marietta, Georgia, on a Saturday night. The sanctuary was filled with family and friends. Billie and I had to turn out the lights and lock the door before we could drive to our reception. OK, maybe some moderate booing and hissing is appropriate.

My incredible parents kept our four children so we could have one night on our own before what became known as "our wedding trip." (We actually had a honeymoon some months later.) We were tired and hungry. I looked out the hotel window and saw the warm glow of a restaurant right across the street. The glow was from the sign at McDonalds. We dined on Big Macs and french fries. I offer no explanation.

The next morning, we picked up our four children, plus a friend for sixteen-year-old John, whom we knew needed a companion besides the three eleven-year-olds. Billie and I, and Scott, Lesley, Melanie, John, and his buddy Kevin, all piled into our Dodge Caravan and headed for the place where I had made reservations for three nights. It was the Gator Motel in downtown Fargo, Georgia.

Please do not gasp out loud.

True enough. We spent three days and nights in the Okefenokee Swamp. We took all our meals at the spacious family-run restaurant next door to our motel. Some people do not think cinder block is adequate for a motel. I think it is just fine. Again, no vegetables thrown!

After that adventure with all our critter friends, we drove to Fernandina Beach, Florida, where I had rented a house on the beach for the last of our spring break adventure.

Edith Ann used to close one of her skits with "And that's the truth." Then followed a great raspberry!

The same goes for me!

WHEN IT WAS FORT BENNING

But you, when you fast, wash your face and groom yourself …

—Matthew 6:17 (CJB)

Fort Benning, near Columbus, Georgia, was a training center for the U.S. Army. Thousands of young men spent about eight weeks there while learning to forget everything and everyone back home. My time began in July 1966.

I was a member of Bravo Company of the Second Battalion of the First Training Brigade. *B 2 1, Sir! Rough! Tough! Argh!* We learned to loudly scream those words, or we would suffer dire consequences.

We had a restaurant in our company area that served delicious meals to about one hundred men three times a day. OK, it was a mess hall, and you were lucky to recognize much of what was being served by scowling faces.

I was thankful for whatever it was we got served. I was a growing twenty-one-year-old. I needed all the protein and vitamins I could find.

But, at no time and under no circumstances were any of us in Company B to approach the food truck that sold hoagie sandwiches and ice-cold soda out the back. That food was probably worth about a dime, but when you have been "voluntold" to fast from all tasty edibles, what are you going to do? It became a nightly challenge for some of us to brave the consequences in order to inhale a hoagie and throw down a giant soda.

His name was Terry. He grew up in Ohio. He was drafted and sent to

Fort Benning. He was one of us. He decided early in life to grow no taller than about five feet. He succeeded in that plan—but he was fast.

He became an official runner from the front steps of our barracks to the hoagie truck and back.

One Thursday evening, just as we were settling in for the night, that tempter called the hoagie truck came to announce its presence. All the officers and sergeants of our company had gone home. The coast was clear. Terry took at least a dozen orders for food, collected the cash, and headed off to the truck.

Little did he know that our company commander, Captain O'Malley, had forgotten something at the mess hall and was circling our area to return home. He spotted the truck. Worse, he spotted Terry, who was clad only in a pair of shorts and a big, white towel.

The captain pulled the front bumper of his car to the point where he touched Terry's towel. Terry froze. He might have been fast, but he was nowhere near fast enough that night.

Captain O'Malley ordered him to throw down the food and then march himself to the area outside the mess hall. Once there, Terry was invited to climb into a wide circle made of sandbags. Inside that circle was about two feet of fresh sawdust. Terry was told to begin low crawling in that pit and to continue crawling until he was told otherwise by someone named "Yes, Sergeant."

We watched Terry disappear into the night with Captain O'Malley. We watched a dozen hoagies and sodas unite into a mess that only a raccoon could love. It would be a long night before our friend Terry could wash his face and groom himself.

THAT SONG AT CAMP GLISSON

|||||||||||||||||||||||||||||||||||||||||||||||||||||||||||||||||||||||||||||||||||||||||||||||||||||||||||||||||||||||||||||||||||||||||||||||||||||||||||||||||||

The prayer of a righteous person is powerful and effective.

—James 5:16 (ISV)

One of the great things about being at church camp at Camp Glisson in North Georgia is the singing—singing in worship, singing in living groups, singing on the porch of the dining hall after supper.

My favorite singing in that lovely place is the song that the camp counselors sing to the campers in the closing worship time. The counselors form a ring around the campers who are seated. Several guitars strike the notes, and the love song begins, "I'll be praying for you every morning, as I start out my day with the Lord …"

Tears are offered all around.

Her name was Margaret. She has gone to heaven now. She could have been the chief operating officer of a number of large companies in the Atlanta, Georgia, area. Instead, she chose a quieter and less prestigious life, yet she lived out her faith in clear and certain ways.

She was my adopted aunt or I was her adopted nephew. I am not sure which. She also adopted my children, John and Lesley, like they were her family. Our birthdays, seasonal holidays, and other ordinary days were all occasions to share food and treats and celebrations with her.

I learned of my pending divorce about the same time I was in the final preparations for my family and me to spend a few months on a pastoral exchange in England. Everyone knew about the trip to England. I told less than a handful of people about the divorce.

I was so proud and stubborn and arrogant that I kept the news from family and friends. I told Margaret the details. Her immediate response was to say, "Why don't we pray?"

She did just that. For the following month, she continued to pray for the children and me every time we met. I confess that I was not really sure what effect those prayers were having, but I was glad she loved us and that she prayed for us.

As I now reflect, her strength was not in her praying with someone. Her gift was in her fervent prayers for someone. I think she would have wept more than she wanted if she had prayed aloud with us.

The divorce was settled on a Friday. The next Monday, we loaded the car with our suitcases and headed for the airport. Margaret had called and asked if we could swing by her apartment in downtown Atlanta on our way to catch our flight. We did.

She was already standing on the sidewalk at the front of her building. I drove up to meet her. She approached the car. She handed me a full manila envelope. She told me that inside were prayers for John, Lesley, and me for the first week of our travels. Once we arrived in England, we would find in the daily mail envelopes filled with prayers for us.

True to her word, there were written prayers for each of us for every day of our journey. The same was true for our time in England. Notes and prayers and encouragement arrived with the morning mail. She also included in the original manila envelope a bundle of cash. She said the money was prayer of a more tangible nature.

One definition of righteous is "the quality of being right in the eyes of God, including character (nature), conscience (attitude), conduct (action), and command (word)."

Under that definition is a small picture of Margaret.

RUTH WAS IN THE CHOIR

> Then the choir that sang and gave thanks took their places
> in God's house. So did I.
> —Nehemiah 12:40 (NIRV, Bowen adaptation)

I was the "Pastor in Charge!" At least, that was what our Book of Discipline called me. I was in my first full-time appointment after graduating from seminary.

The sanctuary of the congregation to which I was appointed had an organ as well as a piano in the building. The choir wore robes. So did I.

The choir sat in rows behind me with a "modesty curtain" between us.

I learned that meant a brass railing in which was hung a curtain of heavy fabric so the congregation could only see the shoulders and heads of the choir when they were seated.

That choir rehearsed every week and prepared wonderful music for our eleven o'clock Sunday morning worship.

The two congregations that I had previously served did not have choirs with robes or modesty rails in their sanctuaries. I felt that in some ways I had arrived. I was now "in charge" of so much, including anthems and special music that was offered before I preached.

I especially liked that Ruth, who sat in the front row of the choir, took copious notes during my sermons. As far as I knew, note-taking had never happened in my other two congregations.

Her attentiveness to my words made me a better preacher. If my attempts at humor fell flat, I could count on Ruth remaining focused on taking her notes.

If I strayed off course and ran too close to twelve noon in my sermon, I knew Ruth was not going to miss a single bit of my third and final point.

The only thing that was negative about being so in charge was a nagging question as to why no one else in the choir ever took a single note during my sermon. I even attended some choir practices to learn if perhaps Ruth was a scribe for the rest of the choir and shared her insights during their rehearsals. That never happened.

It went on for some time—me and Ruth and my sermon and her notes—until the day I decided to lean *way* back as I preached so I could see over the modesty rail and check out what she was writing with such intensity.

My eyes focused on her hands and the pencil and a crossword puzzle book. She was working crossword puzzles as I preached, and everyone in the choir knew it.

I hid this information for a number of years, until I decided to tell the story of Ruth and me and the modesty rail as part of a sermon. My telling brought the desired laughter as a response to the truth that I had never been "in charge" of much at all.

The next Sunday, I was in the middle of preaching and decided to turn and look at the choir, who was seated behind me. As I did, every one of them grinned and held up a crossword puzzle book, and there, leading all that holding and grinning, was Kim, our choir director.

7
WHEN EASTERN AIRLINES FLEW THERE

If I climb upward on the rays of the morning sun ...
—Psalm 139:9 (GWT)

My friends, Ira and Midge, had been assigned to serve the congregation of a church at Islamorada, Florida. They immediately sent word that my children and I were welcome to come for a long visit. What could I say to that?

That plan to visit them was unfolding before Eastern Airlines disappeared.

I sent my children, John and Lesley, to Florida two days before I was able to join them.

My own ticket was booked for an Eastern flight from Atlanta to Miami, where Ira and the kids would meet me for the drive south.

I did not fly enough to qualify for "frequent" anything. I found an early morning flight with a seat in the very last row of the plane. I found my seat, which was the middle of three. After stowing my small bag in the overhead bin, I sat down and buckled in.

My two companions came down the aisle, and after the usual discomforts of dealing with three large men trying to fit into a row of seats designed for the back seat of a Volkswagen Beetle, we got settled in.

I knew that a member of my congregation worked as a flight attendant for Eastern, but I had never been on a flight to which she was assigned.

I had looked for her as I boarded, but I did not see her. As I was looking one more time to see if she was part of our crew, one of my last-row companions began to thumb through a magazine that he had brought aboard. It was basically a hundred pages of pictures and descriptions of small aircraft that were for sale around the country. He thought I would be interested in a picture of and a long monologue about his plane, which was that exact make and model. Only, his plane was fitted out in a more luxurious style.

His words, which bordered on bragging, inspired my other row-mate to start talking about how well he was treated on another airline because he was a titanium mileage holder. It just so happened that his usual carrier did not have a seat available that best suited his busy schedule.

There I was, just a preacher in the last row of a plane trying to get to Miami, Florida, to see my children and my friends.

A person carrying a clipboard while they walk and look around at other people is a powerful thing. And there she was. The member of my congregation was slowly walking from the front of the plane toward us with a clipboard positioned with great authority.

She was checking a list of some kind and nodding to passengers, but never stopped walking. Until she got to us in the last row.

She checked the clipboard one more time and then said, "Mr. Bowen?"

"Yes," I replied.

She said, "On behalf of Eastern Airlines and our flight crew, I want to apologize for any inconvenience you may have experienced with your seat assignment."

She continued, "There was some confusion with boarding, a minor confusion that we have now corrected. If you will come with me, Mr. Bowen, your seat in first class is ready for you." I stood, collected my carry-on, and followed her.

I've played enough tennis to know when game, set, and match are reached.

From where I was going to sit, it would be a gorgeous sunrise.

8

A FAVORITE HYMN

For no other foundation can any one lay than that which
is laid, which is Jesus Christ.

—1 CORINTHIANS 3:11 (RSV)

There are two congregations that are about a mile apart. They are on the same highway, and they have the same names, except one is named Philadelphia Church Number 1, while the other is named Philadelphia Church Number 2. You can drive that highway for yourself and check it out.

I am, by nature, a curious soul. I saw there were two cars in the parking lot at Church 1. I went to the church office and knocked. The door was opened by a pleasant person who asked if I needed something.

I explained that I was a pastor and that I was fascinated by the two congregations that were so close together, yet both kept almost the same name for themselves. There was a pause.

"Music," was the reply.

"How did that happen?"

"Our congregation wanted to keep the music very traditional. We wanted to stay with the hymns as they are written in the hymnal. We did not need any of this contemporary music. That other church insisted on reaching a generation of people who did not like the old hymns. They are still wrong. So, we split."

"Wow," was all I could manage.

I came up with something. May I try it on you and see if it works?

Number 1: All music is contemporary from the day it is first written.

Number 2: All music is traditional the day after it is written.

I loved the music at pastors' school. Several hundred clergy from across Georgia would meet for a few days at a retreat center for worship and fellowship. Some pastors, like me, do not have strong voices for solos and the leading of hymns. Others, whom you may know, are gifted with amazing voices.

One of the greatest gifts at pastors' school comes when those hundreds of voices find the joy of a melody and give their hearts to it. Many are capable of harmony as the hymn rushes to the rafters and thunders there.

It was so that one year. The preacher for the event was from the Midwest. He was "full grown" with a great voice to match his stature.

We sat spellbound and so blessed at the end of his sermon. Then, he reached back into the hymns of the church and began to read. He did not sing. Instead, he read the words of "How Firm a Foundation."

Do you know that one?

It begins with a statement of faith. Then, the words become the words of our God who is pouring reassurance and comfort and peace through those words.

"Fear not …"

"I'll strengthen thee, help thee and cause thee to stand …"

"Through deep waters …"

"Through fiery trials …"

"I will not … desert …"

Finally, as he read the last line of that hymn, his voice reached to share a testimony and to dare us to believe with him and to live out the words.

"That soul, though all hell should endeavor to shake,

I'll never, no, never, no, never forsake."

Instead of reading it as it is printed above, he read it this way: "I'll never, no, never, no, never, no, never, no, never, no, never, no, never, no, never forsake!"

We were later to learn that he was suffering from an incurable disease even as he preached and as he read that hymn for us.

He died within that year.

I believed every word that he preached that day. I believed every word of that hymn that he read that day.

I believe that he ended that last verse exactly the way it should have been.

Sometimes it is good that we cannot tell the difference between contemporary and traditional. Those kinds of words just get in the way.

DAVID G. BOWEN

9

A FUNERAL IN FORT VALLEY, GEORGIA

As he came near the entrance to the city, he met a funeral procession.

—LUKE 7:12 (GWT)

Have you ever seen a job description for a pastor?

They exist. John Wesley was more than explicit in his expectations for those who would serve under their call as a Methodist minister. The Book of Discipline has several pages that outline what is expected of anyone who serves in that capacity.

One of the things I learned from my father about being a Pastor is not written down. He believed that any minister worth her or his salt attended the funerals of anyone in the immediate family of a member of the congregation that minister was serving.

Can you imagine doing that while serving a large membership church?

He knew it to be true, and I believed him.

I had been appointed to the congregation only a few weeks when the father of one of the members died. The funeral was set for an early weekday afternoon at the Methodist church in Fort Valley, Georgia.

I was busy changing schedules when my phone rang. It was a man in the congregation with whom I was already becoming friends. He was calling to offer me a ride with him to that funeral. Would I like to ride with him?

Absolutely!

He picked me up at the church office with plenty of time for an easy ride to the church.

Middle and South Georgia highways are designed so there are long stretches of road with small hills and then miles of not-so-much in between. We were on one of those roads.

Our conversation was light. We joked a bit. We talked about this and that as the miles clicked off. Suddenly, he looked down at the instrument panel of his wife's SUV in which we are riding.

"We are going to be out of gas."

Sure enough, he was a prophet much sooner than I would have wanted.

We coasted to the side of the road and figured I would catch a ride as soon as possible.

It was not soon. It was not possible.

The traffic on that usually busy highway was halted in both directions due to what must have been a cataclysmic event. We prayed for any survivors and then we prayed for a ride to appear.

I heard the truck approaching several miles before it pulled up to us. The cement mixer was clean, and the driver was friendly. He asked if he could help. My friend said he was going to stay with the car but asked if the man could drop me off at Fort Valley Methodist Church for a funeral.

The driver said he would be honored to help a preacher get to a funeral.

I deadlifted myself up the giant staircase into the truck and buckled in for the ride.

The noise at take-off was like a jet-powered Huey with the doors wide open. The driver worked through dozens of gears as we rolled like a tank down the highway. We shouted some words in some language to pass the miles.

I figured I would be let off somewhere near the church. I was wrong. My new best friend, the driver, insisted on taking me right to the front door of that church. We were a few minutes late for the funeral to begin. I was quietly celebrating some anonymity as we approached the church.

The timing could not have been better. As we pulled to an air-braked, screeching halt, the family was just getting out of their limos and other cars at the front sidewalk of the sanctuary. The funeral directors looked between amusement and horror at such an arrival.

I shrunk myself to the size of a Methodist amoeba and slung what was left of my dignity to the street as I exited the truck. I thanked the driver, who could have waited until the family and friends had entered the building, but he had miles to go before he poured cement, so he took off down the runway of Fort Valley, Georgia, and lifted into the afternoon sun.

I mooched a ride to the cemetery after the service at the church. The conversation in that car allowed me to relive my noisy ride all over again.

At the cemetery, I met my buddy, who had managed to get a full tank of gasoline, so we could safely return home.

He grinned and asked, "So, how was the ride down?"

I knew it would appear in a book.

CLERGY TIMES SIX

> Yet who knows—maybe it was for a time like this that
> you are here!
> —ESTHER 4:14 (GNT, BOWEN ADAPTATION)

You never know what is important to someone else. The representative from my congregation was meeting with the bishop of our area to discuss me and my future appointment. My rep had outlined my decades-long commitment to and my involvement in Camp Glisson, Disciple Bible Study, and the Walk to Emmaus. These are all ministries in our local region of North Georgia.

The bishop never hesitated before he said, "Am I supposed to be impressed by David's involvement in these?" Apparently, the bishop was interested in my commitment to another list that did not include these three—or what he perceived to be a lack of commitment on my part.

I have already told you about my love for Camp Glisson. Disciple Bible Study remains one of the best introductory courses that I ever taught. Perhaps I will tell a Bible study story a bit later. That brings us to the Walk to Emmaus.

Emmaus is an ecumenical retreat experience for the building up of local church leaders. I first became involved in Emmaus in 1987. My friend, Roger, had called me to lead a group of five clergy for an Emmaus Walk in the fall of 1995. I was delighted and told him I would begin working to put that team of clergy together.

The first four ministers I called all agreed to serve, and we began our weekly meetings to prepare for that weekend. Then, Roger called me with an unusual request.

He said that God was leading him to ask Ken Kulp to serve with us. He knew that Ken had been a clergy on my own weekend.

I hesitated a bit because we had five clergy committed to serve. I had set up a schedule for these ministers, a schedule with very little room for anyone else. Roger was persuasive, so I finally agreed. I loved Ken and I knew how blessed I was when he served on my Emmaus Walk.

The weekend arrived, and all six clergy began the Walk with my schedule in hand. My primary role was to give a talk on Saturday morning on the "Means of Grace," a term from John Wesley that includes most of the spiritual practices like prayer, Bible study, and Holy Communion. Thursday and Friday went smoothly. I was able to move schedules around so that Ken became a true part of the clergy team.

I was awakened early Saturday morning by a panic attack that was unlike anything I had ever experienced. I could not breathe. I could not speak. I was disoriented and stumbled about my room trying to find any sense as to what was happening.

I located my watch and noted that the time was 2:33 a.m.

Through medical records, I later discovered that was the day and time that our daughter Lesley had fallen to the ground at Hard Labor Creek State Park and had died there.

In the early morning of that Emmaus weekend, I knew none of this. I managed to return to sleep and awoke to my routine of preparing to give a talk. I had dressed and was awaiting the call to make my way to the conference room and share the Means of Grace with the company that would be gathered.

I looked out a window and saw my wife and two friends walking toward the building in which I was quartered. I laughed at the grace of a wife and friends who would drive for miles just to hear me.

Until I saw Billie's face. They entered my room, and upon seeing Billie, I dropped to the floor and yelled, "It's one of our children. Which one is it?"

She told me that Lesley was dead and that we needed to go home.

There are no guidelines or rules for how you receive such a message. My first thought was a strange one. *Who will give the Means of Grace?* was what came to my mind.

Then, clarity poured. *Ken Kulp has served as Head of Clergy on dozens of Emmaus weekends. He knows the talk. He can have my copy if he needs it.*

I packed my gear and climbed into our friend's car to begin the long journey into the worst nightmare of my life.

Thank you, Ken!

DAVID G. BOWEN

DID YOU KNOW YOU WERE AN ANSWER?

You are young, but do not let anyone treat you as if you
were not important.

—1 TIMOTHY 4:12 (ICB)

I had long dreamed of being a father. At the same time, I was frightened of the awesomeness of being one. That may sound familiar to you. The fulfillment of my dream came on June 21, 1973, with the birth of my beloved son, John Dylan, at Emory University Hospital in Atlanta, Georgia. A second fulfillment of my dream, came with the arrival of my beloved daughter, Lesley Ayn, on January 19, 1979, at Crawford Long Hospital in Atlanta, Georgia.

I am a man who loves words, but I was speechless when I got to hold these precious children. My life was changed by the gift of their births.

There were circumstances and decisions that resulted in my understanding that I would never be a father to any children but John and Lesley. I accepted this as a reality for my life. I was saddened.

Several years after my divorce, a remarkable woman named Billie came into my life. We were first acquaintances. We became good friends. Then, we were married on April 8, 1989. I brought the gifts of John and Lesley to our marriage. Billie brought the gifts of Scott Wesley and Melanie Erin. We began the lifelong journey of being a blended family. I continue to be blessed by Scott and Melanie's presence in my life.

Scott and Melanie each found love and the person with whom they would have their own children. To our surprise and great joy, we became grandparents. Melanie and Jerry brought Kayla Brianna and Joshua Sean into our growing family.

Billie and I were privileged to spend a great deal of time with Kayla and Josh, especially on our annual trips to the beach for the Christmas holidays. These two grandchildren lovingly dubbed us as their "Grandma" and "Gramps," names that we celebrate to this day.

The blessings for us were not finished. Scott and Kaelin brought Noah Wesley, Reagan Marie, and Hannah Rose as additions to the family tree. After my retirement in 2017, Billie and I moved our home from Commerce, Georgia, to Cumming, Georgia, so that we might be more fully involved in the lives of these grandchildren.

We were also given name changes by Noah. He would probably have a better explanation for the names, but this is my story. As soon as he began to speak, he decided and then he announced that we were to be "Mooma" and "Poopa." No, you read that correctly.

Our first grandparent names are readily accepted by spellchecker as authentic and acceptable. Our second set still registers as unacceptable, underlined by bright-red squiggles. Who cares?

Billie Rose: I love you and I honor you as my helpmeet!

John, Lesley, Scott, Melanie, Jerry and Kaelin: I am so blessed by you!

Kayla, Josh, Noah, Reagan, and Hannah: I am so proud of you!

Each of you is an answer to my prayers and to my dreams!

I STAND LIKE THEM AT CHRISTMAS—A POEM

Therefore the Lord himself will give you a sign: behold, a virgin shall conceive, and bear a son, and shall call his name Immanuel.

—ISAIAH 7:14 (ASV)

I stand like them at Christmas:
The hurting, hungry ones.

The bread and drink not so much as a word of Hope!
Hope … here and now.
As I am in hopelessness,
As I am in sorrow,
As I am in disease,
As I am in death.
Oh, God, speak to me of that hope!

I stand like them at Christmas:
The faithful ones, bowed with watching
And waiting,
Straining the skies and all beyond
For some bright glimpse that joins us to God.

I stand like them at Christmas:
The searching ones, heavy with the journey

From place to place,
From escape to escape,
Only to find I brought myself along
And God is with us still.

I stand like them at Christmas,
Beholding the angel voices
That reach amid the dying ones,
Sharing the baby's birth
That heals all broken wounds.

I stand like them at Christmas,
Yearning for a voice to speak
Joy in this day and time for you.
Living at times afraid that God
Might forget,
Might have forgotten.
And doubting, I build high houses of power and might.
But I am alone in such.

I stand like them at Christmas
Waiting, watching, yearning for some word …
And it is

Immanu'el
With us, God!

MARSHA WAS MARRIED TO RANDY

> Therefore confess your sins to each other and pray for each other so that you may be healed. The prayer of a righteous person is powerful and effective.
>
> —James 5:16 (NIV)

Randy adopted me as his duck-hunting partner. His wife, Marsha, taught school. I felt a connection of spirit with her, but our relationship consisted of "hello" and "goodbye" as Randy I were off to the swamps.

We didn't have a truck. His retriever was lazy. We never imagined that we would ever get close to our limit on ducks. We used our hunting as a good way to be out and doing guy stuff.

One of our favorite spots for finding wood ducks and mallards is now a massive intersection on Georgia Highway 400 North at the McFarland Road exit. Back in our day, it was a small, paved country road with a barely scraped dirt trail off to the right that led down to a swamp-haven for ducks.

One of my least favorite days with Randy was our trip out to this swamp in Marsha's station wagon. We made the ride down that dirt trail and to the parking place without a hitch. During the several hours we duck hunted, it rained a lot. Imagine a huge station wagon trying to move up a muddy dirt road with tires spinning and mud being slung all over the place.

Additional RPMs only increased the spinning and the slinging. Worse, the car wanted to slide off the mud road into a ditch on the right side.

We were stuck at least seven ways to Sunday.

We finally decided that I would place myself between the side of the massive car and the wall of the ditch. Randy was to accelerate slowly so the tires would try to grab the dirt under the mud. Meanwhile, I would push the spinning-tired vehicle away from the ditch so we might make some progress back toward McFarland Road.

There is a website featuring "why women live longer than men," but I do not think it is appropriate to mention it here.

It worked. Despite all the ways it should have been a miserable, muddy failure, our spin and shove worked.

Randy was an excellent sales rep for his company. He was so good that he was moved to Arkansas to manage a territory. I said a sad goodbye to Randy and Marsha.

Several years later, my marriage was coming to a sliding halt. After a long night, my wife agreed that she would be the one who told our children, eleven-year-old John and five-year-old Lesley, that our marriage was ending.

The children and I were seated on the sofa in our great room. I sat between the kids. I had an arm around each of them as my wife broke the terrible news to them.

The next day rose uneasily.

About mid-morning, I received a phone call from a number that I did not recognize.

It was Randy's wife. It was Marsha.

She said, "I was praying this morning, and I was given a troubling sight.

I saw you on a sofa with your arms around John and Lesley and you were all weeping. David, what has happened?"

I told her. As we wept and prayed together, I understood one way that powerful and effective might look.

14

Y'ALL GET IN THE CAR

|||||||||||||||||||||||||||||||||||||||||||||||||||||||||||||||||||||||||||||||||||||||||||||||||||||||||||||||||||||||||||||||||||||||||||||||||||||||||||||||||||||

For which of you, desiring to build a tower, does not first,
having sat down, count the cost, whether he has *enough*
for *its* completion?

—LUKE 14:28 (BLB)

Do you remember those family trips when you were a child? I recall the rides to our grandparents' home in Athens, Georgia. The ride took a short time. We were all awake for the entire trip.

It was different when we traveled to Panama City, Florida, to Aunt Gloria's house. The three of us children would fall asleep in our own beds and wake up the next morning in Florida. It took years for me to figure out how my parents made that happen. Once there, we would also find our other grandparents and lots of cousins, aunts, and uncles who had also gathered for holidays.

But the great magic journey came in the year our family of five went to Washington, DC, for the long-awaited visits to monuments, museums, and national treasures. We stayed in a building called a motel for a night. Can you imagine how wonderfully strange that was for me?

Even better, we had breakfast in a restaurant. I met my first serving of Canadian bacon and have never fallen out of love.

I wanted to move into the Smithsonian and forever play among the dinosaurs and soar with the airplanes suspended from the ceilings. President Lincoln was huge in his thoughtful chair. I looked for President

Washington in his monument, but all I saw was a tall set of stairs. Our trip was better than I ever expected.

My greatest joy was a building not yet finished. We drove up a long hill and there it was, Washington National Cathedral.

I noticed that there was a school on the grounds of that building. If a person can intellectually drool, then that is what I did that afternoon. All my being was drawn to the massive stone pieces that were scattered around the grounds. I learned that the cathedral was being finished as funds became available. I further learned that the pieces I saw on the ground were parts of the two great towers which were yet to be placed against the sky.

When we left Washington, I left part of me at the cathedral. My subscription to National Geographic Magazine kept me up to date as the building continued to rise.

I was not able to return until May 2004, when I donned my robe in the basement of that now-completed wonder and walked the aisle to receive the doctorate that I had earned.

Thank you, Mom and Dad, for the journey!

DAVID G. BOWEN

OUT OF THE MOUTHS OF EARLY TEENS

The fear of the LORD is the beginning of wisdom.
—PROVERBS 9:10 (GWT)

My father spent forty-seven years on active duty as a Methodist preacher. Therefore, I was a "preacher's kid." I grew up with that said about me. Some people never cared to find out a single thing about me. They knew everything worth knowing with that label for me.

Later, I was told that a more correct nickname for folks like me was "theological offspring." It just does not have quite the ring, does it?

A few minutes ago, I made up another one. I am going to call myself and others like me "parsonage progeny."

My Bible knowledge was less than weak in my youth and childhood. I could get out something like "Jesus wept" or "God is love." Beyond the range of those, I was a lost cause.

Worse, I misunderstood Bible passages. I memorized the Twenty-third Psalm for my grandfather. I wear his name, George, as a part of mine.

That psalm opens with: "The Lord is my shepherd, I shall not want." That is a great opening line for anything biblical. *My* problem was that I heard it like this: "The Lord is my shepherd and I do not want Him to be."

Woe to any preacher's kid who might think like that.

With that kind of poor biblical background, can you imagine the terror in my heart when I was applying to attend seminary and to serve as a local pastor?

Right now, I need to offer a word of apology and sincere thanks to those congregations who received me as their pastor when I did not know Jehoshaphat from Jerusalem—a word of apology and sincere thanks!

I suffered from biblical ignorance. I suffered from biblical misunderstanding. I think the most frightening thing about me was that I would speak up in church if the preacher asked what sounded like a question.

I have been told by certifiable sources that a good preacher or pastor does not ever tell a story that involves any of their family from the pulpit, or the podium, or the lectern.

Those same sources told me that you should avoid having those same family members raise their hand to answer a question that you might pose to your congregation. I tried to honor both those bits of wisdom.

Until that Sunday morning in East Cobb County, Georgia. The day was bright and crisp. The sanctuary was filled. The music was strong. My text was the title to this story. In a moment of clarity or something else, I stopped my sermon and asked those folks, "Can anybody tell me what 'fear of the Lord' means?"

It turned out that many of my congregation were like me. They had also grown up with merely a modicum of biblical knowledge. I did not panic at the silence or at the eyes cast away from me looking for an answer to my question. My anxiety did begin to rise when I noticed that the only hand raised in that church house was the hand of my beloved son, John.

I was like an auctioneer who is not satisfied with the last bid and begins to yell: "Is there another?" Silence and un-raised hands were the responses of my people. You finally reach a point, don't you?

I looked up as if I was seeing John and his hand for the first time. I looked up as if I had expected him alone and no one else to offer an answer to my question. I said, "John, did you have an answer?"

"Yes, Dad," he replied. "Did you ask: 'What does "fear of the Lord" mean?'"

"I did" were the words I chose in some fear and trembling.

DAVID C. BOWEN

"'Fear of the Lord' means totally awesome respect," John said with authority.

The sermon was over. It was time for the closing hymn and the Benediction.

16

CHURCH WARS

> I know your works: you are neither cold nor hot. Would
> that you were either cold or hot! So, because you are
> lukewarm, and neither hot nor cold, I will spit you out
> of my mouth.
>
> —REVELATION 3:15–16 (ESV)

Temperature settings on thermostats have long been a source of either
suffering or amusement in local congregations. There are hints of such
ecclesiastical squabbles in the Scriptures. I have not only heard of such
things, but I have witnessed them in person.

The one church that I served had a single thermostat on the back wall
of the sanctuary. It had a clear plastic cover that could not be locked. There
were several members of the congregation who could never tolerate the
temperature as it had been set by another member.

I sat behind the pulpit, from which I could easily see the thermostat
and all those who thought a reset was in order. Worship would have
barely begun as a shadowy figure moved to the back wall and flipped the
temperature down because they were totally burning up.

Moments later, another shadowy figure moved and flipped the
temperature back up because they were freezing to death.

We were fortunate during my first year that neither skulker died during
the eleven o'clock worship hour. I must have been the lukewarm person in
the Bible, because I never got too warm or too cold. I was mostly just right.

DAVID G. BOWEN

I was not immune from messing with those folks. During one long weekend, I hired an electrician to place a new thermostat in a closet at the rear of the sanctuary.

That closet could be secured with a lock. I also had the old thermostat left in place with its plastic cover and worn-out settings. Each Sunday morning, I would arrive and set the temperature on the thermostat in the closet to my liking. The fun came as shadowy figures moved throughout the morning to get the air in the room to the degree they wanted. They never succeeded.

I served another church that had more visible temperature skirmishes. They were because the thermostat was on the wall to the right of the choir. That meant the settings were in plain sight of the entire congregation. Therefore, anyone moving to change the settings was visible to one and all.

He must have been born with low blood, or his personal internal thermostat was never hooked up. We didn't print this in the morning bulletin so people would notice. We didn't need to, because every Sunday during the time to move and greet one another, he came across the choir and defiantly shoved that temperature to low boil.

Just as regularly, one of the choir members would move to ease the temperature back to some range of normalcy.

The rest of the story came after we had moved from there to serve another congregation.

This thermostat control steward wore a flannel shirt that was about four inches thick. It was his extra layer of warmth because the earth never had a temperature that suited him. The church was having a yard sale with tables of items for purchase. He came to the sale. He saw an outer garment that he wanted to add to his collection. He removed the famous flannel shirt to try on the other coat.

While he was doing the try-on thing, someone sold his flannel shirt to a passer-by. 'Nuff said.

17

EARS TO HEAR

Doctor, make yourself well!

—Luke 4:23 (EasyEnglish Bible)

I was blessed and honored to serve three years on active duty in the US Army. Let's put aside all the political stuff that could separate us and be at peace with our pasts. Is that acceptable to you?

After basic training at the lovely retreat center of Fort Benning, Georgia, I was sent to Fort McClellan, Alabama, for additional training. My next stop was back to Fort Benning, where I was a member of the Human Resources and Research Organization (HumRRO), which was attached to the infantry school. I was then sent to Germany, where I served as part of the Military Hygiene and Counseling Services (MHCS) at an airbase near Kitzingen, Germany.

I give you all this information to bring you to my last few months in Germany.

Our MHCS Clinic was being closed for a major renovation of the facility. We were out of a job for a few months. I wanted to do more than hang around the army post for what time I had left in the service.

The army hospital in a nearby city was looking for an enlisted soldier to assist the psychiatrist with daily rounds on the wards. The person would basically do anything Major Jess Groesbeck, the Third Infantry Division Psychiatrist, wanted them to do. That sounded like my kind of job description.

I was accepted into the position. I rode a dull-green army bus for the half-hour trip each day. My grandchildren called their yellow bus "The Big Cheese."

I suppose that, in keeping with them, I rode on "The Big Olive."

I got to carry a clipboard as I walked beside Dr. Groesbeck to visit hospitalized enlisted personnel as well as a few military dependents. I was fascinated to serve with this very bright man. We shared some personal stories during our rounds. I thoroughly enjoyed my work with him.

One day, he stopped walking down the hall. He turned to me and said, "David, you do an excellent job of working with the pain and suffering of others. When will you begin to work with your own pain?"

I was convinced at that moment that I would spend the rest of my life in the field of mental health and psychiatry. I came close, didn't I?

Thank you, Jess, for your incredible patience and for encouraging me to become a member of the salt.

18

FIRST YEAR OF SEMINARY

A wise person is careful to keep away from trouble. But a foolish person is careless and he thinks that he is always right.

—PROVERBS 14:16
(EASYENGLISH BIBLE, BOWEN ADAPTATION)

There is a warning that a person who has attended a seminar or a conference is most dangerous when they first get back home.

That was doubly true of me in my first class in pastoral care in seminary. I had attended one or two classes. I became convinced that I was an expert in offering pastor-like compassion to hurting people.

A relative of a member of the congregation I was serving had been admitted to the hospital with the diagnosis of a very serious condition.

She had anorexia nervosa. I went by the hospital on my way home from class to visit her.

Her appearance stunned me. You can read about an illness or a sickness in a textbook, but meeting face to face with human suffering is a rather different thing.

I was armed with a plastic name badge and all the experiences of one week of being a pastor. I boldly found her room and knocked on the door to ask if I could enter.

This was not her first hospitalization, nor was this her first time to encounter a careless adult who was "going to help her."

DAVID G. BOWEN

It would have been good for me to gently express the concern of her family and our congregation and then leave after a brief prayer. That type of visit would have had the lovely aroma of wisdom.

Instead, I became a trial lawyer for some medieval inquisition. I bombarded her with questions about a dozen subjects, none of which were any of my business. She remained very quiet and stared at me.

Finally, she said, "Preacher, I am not in this hospital to be the subject of some analysis that you think you are entitled to throw on me. I am not well. I am struggling to stay alive. I need help. But you are not here to make me feel better. You care only about figuring out something in my family history that brought me here. You need to leave."

I did.

And I returned a week later to visit her. She was so gracious to me. It seems that information and humility are gifts from rather different sources.

19

WE WERE AT THE JORDAN RIVER

At this time, Jesus came from Nazareth in Galilee and was baptized by John in the Jordan. The moment he came out of the water, he saw the sky split open and God's Spirit, looking like a dove, come down on him.

—MARK 1:9–10 (THE MESSAGE)

I live in Georgia. We are blessed by water. There are some eighteen major river systems in our state. There are also hundreds of smaller creeks and streams that connect with the major rivers. That is why the water situation in Israel seems so strange to me. Think about it—only one river in an entire country.

One river in Israel. It is not much of a river when you finally see it. On my first visit to Israel, we were crossing the Jordan and I had to ask the bus driver to back up because none of us got a picture. It was that narrow.

But, oh, the stories of and from and about this water.

He was from Memphis, Tennessee. He was full-grown. He asked if I would baptize him in the Jordan. He had waited for this moment, and I was honored to serve as his pastor in one of the most important events of his life.

We had stopped near the lower end of the Sea of Galilee, where the Jordan has been dammed so the current does not sweep away those who are being baptized. The spot has a mandatory gift shop for tourists. Occasionally, a pilgrim will also purchase some goodies for those back home. We secured long, white robes from the shop and made our way down to the water.

Years ago, the nation of Israel planted thousands of eucalyptus trees along the river. They overhung the water where the man and I were entering to celebrate his faith. The trees produce great shade. They are also the resting places for huge, white pigeons. The pigeons normally stay in the trees unless someone is making a food offering. Then, they will visit in droves to eat and to share bird gifts on anyone in the area.

On this day, no one was feeding pigeons, so we were safe. I read Scripture and prayed with the man. We entered the water up to our waists. I had him place a hand over his nose and immersed him in the Jordan. I spoke the ancient words of Baptism.

He burst out of the water, threw his arms toward the heavens, and began to praise God and to thank Jesus. At that moment, one single dove left his eucalyptus tree and sailed right down the river and over our heads. The man opened his eyes and spotted the bird when it was about three feet over us.

He shouted, "Praise the Lord. It is the dove of the Holy Spirit!"

Dove? Pigeon? It is not about the bird, is it? I shouted back to him, "Yes! Praise the Lord!"

On another trip, we returned to that same Jordan River place called the Yardenit Baptism Center. The pigeons were resting in the eucalyptus trees. Billie and I were leading a group, out of which twenty-six wanted to remember their baptism or to be baptized by immersion in the Jordan.

Billie took her place at an overlook so she could take photographs or videos for those celebrating Jesus and the water. We shared Scripture and prayers with our group. I waded out into the river and began to immerse our friends.

I did not see that a woman wearing a hijab had entered the water behind me and had begun to slowly swim away from the shore. There are large ducks that had made the Jordan River their home. They were colored

red, white, and black. Did I mention they were large birds? One of these ducks spotted the woman swimming in its territory and began to water-walk toward her while flapping its wings. The duck landed by the woman and began to beat her on the head and shoulders.

I was not aware of this scene as it unfolded behind me, because I was totally focused on celebrating the baptisms of our group. Billie spotted the woman's encounter with the duck. She captured it on video since it took place directly behind me.

We did not offer the woman a copy of the film. I don't think she would have been very interested.

20

NOT UNLIKE DEATH——A POEM

The LORD bless you and keep you:
The LORD make his face to shine upon you, and be
gracious to you:
The LORD lift up his countenance upon you, and give
you peace.

> —NUMBERS 6:24–26 (RSBV)

I served wonderful congregations as a pastor for forty-three years before I retired. Each of these congregations became like a family to me. Leaving them was painful. I wrote the following to express some of what I felt, but I never fully expressed to them. I do that now.

Not unlike death
comes the leaving of a pastor from a people.
Attempted, muted goodbyes … both of us saying,
"I'll see you,"
although we have only seen one another up to now
as Birnam trees walking.

Oh, Paul, traveler and journeyman!
Your story reads so comfortingly,
yet my heart aches.
You understand.

You know I don't majestically grieve the
congregation's loss of me.

In quieter, more painful confession,
I mourn my loss of you
and all the named faces of all those years.

I am not an appointment
to be arranged, made, and kept,
and I am angry at being treated as such!
You have seen beneath my anger and asked
about the pain lying there.
Thank you.

For my pain-hiding anger will become
less frightening,
and in time, some increase shall be mine,
for not unlike death
comes the leaving of a pastor from a people.

21

BETWEEN DOWNTOWN MARIETTA, GEORGIA, AND HOME

And the food became known as "manna" (meaning "What is it?"); it was white, like coriander seed, and flat, and tasted like honey bread.

—Exodus 16:31 (TLB)

Just because you can't sleep, and you don't eat, and you look like the cat dragged you down sixty-three flights of stairs does not necessarily mean you are depressed.

Like the Bee Gees song, I was "staying alive," but I was not living. I had returned from the summer in England with my children. They were back in school. I was back at work as the pastor of a wonderful congregation in Georgia.

I slept some, but not deeply. I ate some, but I was not being nourished by what I ate. What was I to do? Maybe I should go to see my doctor.

I did. He was kind. Sorta. He asked me how long I had been helping people with their suffering and their ailments. I saw it was a trick question. I answered that it had been a lot of years.

He asked how long I had been going without enough sleep or enough food, but especially how long I had been going without enough rest so I could heal. I answered that it had been several months.

He asked me how long I had been helping other people. I told him I had been doing that for more than twenty years. He began to gently laugh, and he asked when I might catch on that I was suffering from depression and that I needed help. He was right.

He said, "I am prescribing a medicine for you. It will not act immediately on your depression, but it will help you rest so that you and I can deal with your depression. It might take a week or so. Take the meds and get back with me when you feel a result."

That was one of the strangest prescriptions I was ever given. I didn't even bother to look the drug up and find any information about it. I just got the prescription filled and began taking it. At first, I noticed nothing in the way of change.

I continued to serve full-time as pastor of my congregation. One of the ways that I served was to make visits to folks who were in the hospital.

One morning, I drove to Kennestone Hospital in Marietta, Georgia, and visited with several patients and a couple of staff who were also in my congregation.

The road home went by a restaurant called Po Folks. The name was an attempt to draw customers who thought the name indicated some magical Southern food served with a drawl in every bite. They were right on a lot of the food served there.

Atlanta got more sophisticated when the Olympics were scheduled to be held in Georgia, so Po Folks became just Folks.

I pulled in and was seated near the front door because the restaurant was crowded with the lunch bunch. I ordered a simple meal of fried chicken and vegetables. I was prepared to nibble a bit and to taste nothing.

Boy, I was wrong. I smelled that chicken before it got to the table. That was strange because my depression had turned all tastes for me into cardboard. I thanked my server. I began to weep.

I was not doing the crocodile-tears kind of weep, but it was enough to draw my server back to my table.

"Sir, is something wrong with your food?"

"Oh, no," was all I could get out.

He got the manager. By the time that person arrived I was even deeper into my weeping. The manager was concerned. He was mainly concerned because I was disturbing other customers.

I explained that the food smelled so good that it meant I was once again alive and that I would be healed in time.

The manager nodded like he understood. He and my server then moved me and my food and my weeping to the back of the restaurant where there were no other customers.

I joyously ate all my meal. I left an enormous tip as I paid my bill.

To lovingly paraphrase Fred Craddock, that chicken tasted like love and grace and mercy.

THAT ASH WEDNESDAY SERVICE

I repent and mark myself with ashes.

—JOB 42:6 (BOWEN ADAPTATION)

I admit it. I love the seasons of the Christian year.

Our parents introduced the liturgical or church seasons to us. I have followed their outline of time for the rest of my life. I am particularly drawn to the season of Lent. I celebrated that season as a period of preparation so that the suffering and death of Jesus was a place for helping us deal with the same things in our lives.

Additionally, I like the Lenten emphasis on purple and all that it signifies about both royalty and humility. One thing about Lent that was not part of my early life was the imposition of ashes on the forehead as a part of Ash Wednesday. I particularly appreciate the power of Psalm 51 as one of the readings for that service of worship.

Several of the congregations that I served were led in all things worship by a dedicated group called the Altar Guild. These folks took seriously the symbols of the Christian year as well as the preparation of the elements for Ash Wednesday.

They kept the palm branches from Palm Sunday each year. Those fronds were dried and then burned. The ashes from that burning were collected and mixed with anointing oil to provide the ashes for Ash Wednesday.

One year, our congregation was meeting in our chapel for that service.

We sang a hymn or two in a minor key. We shared Psalm 51 as a responsive reading.

As I did every year, I presented the story of how the palm branches from the previous year became the ash mixture that would be placed on our foreheads that evening.

The service went well until I apparently gave too much time and too many details on the burning of the ashes. There was a wonderful young family in worship that night. The couple had their small children in attendance with them.

They were seated several rows from the altar area where our church lay reader and I were placing the ashes on foreheads in the shape of a cross. When the time came for this family to make their way forward to the altar area, their youngest child, a very independent young boy, began to moan and yell in protest.

His mother attempted to calm him. I did not catch every word spoken between them. I do remember the major argument he was presenting that night. "Mom don't let that man put those hot ashes on me! I don't want to get burned up!"

NOT SO MUCH STUDY THAT NIGHT

|||||||||||||||||||||||||||||||||||||||||||||||||||||||||||||||||||||||||||||||||||||||||||||||||||||||||||||||||||||||||||||||||||||||||||||||||||||

First pride, then the crash— the bigger the ego, the harder the fall.

—PROVERBS 16:18 (THE MESSAGE)

They were my friends. They were active in the life of our congregation. I met with Hank on a regular basis in an accountability group. Susie played a mean game of tennis. She was also an animal control officer for an adjoining county.

Susie was born and raised in a family where hard work and honesty were of great value. Hank was not. His family practically owned and operated a small town in Kentucky. That meant his family had established and were the major financial backers and leading laypersons in the Methodist church in his hometown.

Susie worked tirelessly at her profession. A parade of assorted critters met her on the end of her Ketch All and Dual Release Catch Poles. You may have seen these poles on TV. They have a retractable noose of rope on the end of a broomstick. This arrangement of rope and pole protects the animal from harm and keeps the control officer at a safe distance. Susie could be competitive in both her work and her tennis.

Hank worked tirelessly at being some kind of salesman for a major company. He had also fashioned himself as an "influencer" in our local community. That meant his opinion on everything was a lot more important than anyone else's knowledge or opinion. Hank could be annoying.

They both attended and participated in a weekday evening Bible study at our church. About half the time, they got along well and added a great deal to the class. The other half of the time was taken up in either outright argument or semi-snide comments about one another.

One of the usual sources of conflict between them was how important his family was and continued to be in that Kentucky town. She refused to acknowledge that his family's wealth and prestige entitled him to anything more than a place at the table with the rest of us. And on and on they would ride.

One gray night, it happened. There may have been a full moon that evening, so lunacy might have been stirring. A storm front might have been approaching, so all the animals may have been restless. At any rate, both Susie and Hank showed up for Bible study on the edge of a soap opera that would be played out before us.

I welcomed the members of the class and asked if anyone had anything to share before we began our reading and discussion. Susie raised her hand.

"Hank," she said. "Did you get the mail before you came tonight?"

"Of course, I did. I always get the mail."

"Well, Hank," she continued. "Was the newspaper in the mail?"

"Of course. I always check to make sure we got our paper."

"Did you by chance read any of the paper?"

"Of course. I always read the paper, starting with the sports section."

"Well," she added, "Did you look at the want ads?"

By this time, we were all about to bust out of our seats with both anticipation and dread. We anticipated Susie's next words. We dreaded the effect of those next words on Hank.

Hank answered sharply, "No, I did not read the want ads. They have nothing in which I am interested in the least. Why do you ask?"

We all gasped.

"I just wondered if you had read the want ad where you found that the angel Gabriel had died and you have been put in charge of the earth."

GEORGE DARDEN, YOUR FATHER, HAD DIED—A POEM

And Isaac breathed his last, and he died and was gathered
to his people, old and full of days. And his sons Esau and
Jacob buried him.

—GENESIS 35:29 (ESV)

I drove that long road from Atlanta down to Sparta, Georgia.

It seems there are almost as many memories as there are pine trees along the highway.

I could not remember the turn-off toward the area we called the Shoals, but my heart felt its way as I followed the hearse with your father's body inside.

The old, red dirt road is tar-covered now. Perhaps not so much out of shame and embarrassment as out of consideration for car springs and tires.

The blackberries are red. The doves sit in audience on the power lines. There is an early afternoon haze as far as the eye can see.

The plums hang like red-orange ornaments on a Christmas tree. Plum pits have been spit and tossed out pick-up truck windows, from wagon seats, and from children's sweet hands.

Plum bushes have sprung up thicket-like along the roadside. They have thorns, but these sharp points only produce braggable wounds of independence. They do not permanently scar.

I imagine that I can hear the moos of the dairy cattle on your folk's place. The fields are now greened over and the cows long gone. The barns and sheds have leaned so far that they have been taken down.

Without effort, I return to early summer morning with the sounds and smells of your mom's breakfast. You allowed me to pretend that I had helped you with early-dark chores so that I could sit at her table. No meal since has come close to the nourishing standards she set or to the love that she gave in that food.

The creek water was always cooler than the sweat that covered us. We swung on ropes draped from trees until fire-fly dark called us to the house.

The sun bouncing off the hearse hurts my eyes. Sunglasses reflect some of that harsh light. My eyes really burn from my tears.

We are burying your father. The Baptist churchyard is filled with trucks and cars like Homecoming Sunday in June. Family and friends have driven from all over the South to share in standing with you and remembering.

George Darden is his name. A marker will spell out his dates for those who later come to visit and to look.

You and your family do so well with the huge crush of touching people. We speak words to you. I suspect you know that we really don't know what to say to you, but we speak anyway. You are gracious to receive us and to hear our hesitant words.

I have to leave now.

The ride to my home will be long. I leave the churchyard and turn onto the highway back toward Sparta. The afternoon has collected all the heat from the earlier hours and beats down on my car.

I pass the fields and farms now sweltering in the Georgia sun. I cross the creek over a cement bridge and strain to hear children at play in that cool water.

Suddenly, I pull to the side of the road. There is a row of loaded plum trees up the hill to the side of the pavement. I slide and climb sideways on the red dirt and reach up through the thorns to pick enough plums to fill my hat.

Standing by the side of the road I eat sun-heated memories.
I think of fathers.
I think of children.
I think of us.
I taste, and I weep, and I laugh.

DAVID G. BOWEN

25

WON'T GET MUCH BETTER

They went and got into the boat, but that night they didn't catch anything.

—John 21:3 (TCJB)

My family tree did not branch out far. We are more like the tough, resilient bristlecone pine than a stand of quaking aspens. The limbs are tough. The leaves are strong. One of my frustrations about modern life is the distance we live from one another. This has always been true for my cousins. We saw each other far too many times at funerals or at the bedside of someone who was not well.

I did have that one night and day with my cousin, Don. He and I wanted to go deep-sea fishing. Our usual choice was to secure a place with one of the boats of Captain Anderson. His fleet was based in Saint Andrews near Panama City, Florida.

The collective wisdom of dads and uncles prevailed. We would have better luck leaving from further West. We contacted a fleet out of Destin, Florida. We would be able to board our vessel about "o' dark thirty," and we could fish far longer with that early start. Plans were made. Tickets were bought. Transportation was set.

Don and I arrived in Destin and found seats inside the cabin near the galley. We noticed the absence of other fishermen. We asked if others would be joining us. We were told that the rest were already on board. They had purchased bunks below deck so they could sleep on their way to the fishing grounds. They had also been partying "hearty" all evening. The noises coming from below told us the party was not finished.

The boat eased from the dock, and we were underway. Our partying companions quieted down.

Don and I talked and dozed off for a few hours. He had brought his portable chess set. I was pretty sure that we were among the very few deep-sea fishing dudes who played chess in the galley of a boat.

Morning broke clear and crisp. One of the crew also served as the chief cook and bottle washer. We were hungry, and the smell of breakfast called to us. Our boat was wave-dancing on the swells. I began to reason that folks who had partied all night might not be calmed by the movement, nor would they be soothed by the scent of bacon and eggs in the early morning. I was right.

As Don and I ate egg and bacon sandwiches, figures from the deck below began to stagger into the light and find places at the railing of the boat. They were not fishing. They were not going to be fishing.

Don and I had bought a place in the contest with a cash reward for the person who caught the largest red snapper on the trip. Our shadowy companions had also entered the same contest. Things were looking good for our chances.

You can guess the rest of the story. We had the railing to ourselves. We picked the best spots to plug in our electric reels. We had the entire supply of cigar minnows that snappers love. They are so much better than the cut-up squid that we ordinarily would have been handed.

Cousins finish first. We caught the biggest Red Snapper and claimed that prize. We filled up four five-gallon lard cans with filets. We rode home in triumph. As for our shadowy companions, they didn't catch anything—but we did! Love ya, Don. Love ya, family!

26

UNDERWRITTEN BY GRACE

You will be made rich in every way so that you may be generous in every way, which produces thanksgiving to God through us.

—2 Corinthians 9:11 (EHV)

I was lost. I was out of the army. I had completed my undergraduate degree at Georgia State University. I was working full-time at Sears on Ponce de Leon Avenue in Atlanta. It was right after the Thanksgiving madness of dealing with the public in a retail business. We were hiring part-time associates for the Christmas holidays in men's wear.

His name is C. R. Hill. There are other names that follow those two consonants, but he prefers C. R. He was also an army vet. He was attending the Candler School of Theology at Emory University while serving a small membership Methodist congregation in the North Georgia foothills. We began to have lunch together and to share our life stories.

I cannot tell you the day or the time. I know it was in early December. I can tell you that C. R. began to gently encourage me to fulfill my dream of finding healing for myself and a way to serve God. I would not have used that kind of language, because I was thinking about a career and profession. I was not yet thinking in ways that were connected to Jesus and his call on my life.

Clarity is often given to those who would knock and ask and seek. I began to listen to both C. R. and God. Or, perhaps better, to God and to C. R. The logical next step for me was to apply to Candler. I was not as clear as to what that might entail. Or how I was to pay for that education. Or …

I called Candler and began the process of receiving an application so that I might attend. I was given a date and a time to bring that completed application to Candler. We were given the gift of a snowy ice storm the day before I was to apply. Roads were drivable, but not up any of the long hills surrounding Emory University. I drove as far as I could get and then walked about a half mile to the campus.

The person in charge of "all things that really matter" had fought her own way to the Candler offices. She was completely surprised that I had trudged in such icy weather to keep my appointment. The person with whom I was to meet was not available, but she took my application and commended my persistence on getting accepted to Candler.

I had attended several colleges and universities in the years before my time at Georgia State. I asked that my transcripts be forwarded to Candler. My application was handed in, my transcripts received. I waited.

The phone call I was expecting came while I was at work at Sears. It was not the call for which I had hoped. It was a person from the admissions office at Candler. He appreciated my sincerity in making the application. However, my grades were not acceptable for graduate school in theology.

I was stunned. I had no response, until I remembered that my transcripts would have been several pages in length. Jokingly, I have told people that my first two years of college left me with a negative grade point average. They usually reply that such is impossible. I leave the conversation at that. I asked the man if he had looked on the back of the transcripts. He had not. I knew that I had earned nearly all "A's" during my last three years at Georgia State. There was a long pause as I waited.

He laughed. Lord, have mercy, he laughed. So did I. C. R. and I celebrated. He knew what a life-changing thing I had done. I did not. I was to learn.

I was accepted and began my journey into seminary and into the ministry. One question remained for me: How would I pay for this?

I had about a year left on the G.I. Bill, but that amount would never cover my expenses for the next several years. I made my way back to Candler to discuss my plight.

The same woman who was at Candler on that snowy, icy, December day was again in her office. We exchanged pleasantries. I was just starting to pour out my story of great need when she stopped me. She said that I was beginning seminary in January, so some scholarships that had not been available in the fall term were now offered. Was I interested in a full scholarship for my time at Candler? I wept. "Yes."

A family in Atlanta had been able to pour financial generosity into the lives of several seminary students each year. I was one of those blessed students. I had thanksgiving to God for this family. I had the encouragement and love of C. R. I had the support and prayers of my family. I had the guidance of at least two of the staff at Candler.

The doors were no longer shut. The shutters on the windows were thrown open. I was as clearly bathed in grace as anyone who has ever lived. Thanks be to God!

27

LOOKING FOR A HOME

||||||||||||||||||||||||||||||||||||||||||||||||||||||||||||||||||||||||||||||||||||||||||||||||||||||||||||||||||||||||||||||||||||||||||||

> Go from your country and your kindred and your father's
> house to the land that I will show you.
>
> —GENESIS 12:1 (ESV)

My family is comprised of people of every size and shape you can imagine. We are probably very much like your family in that regard, but we are short on written records and documents that would give us lots of pictures of our heritage.

I know that we had ancestors who fought with George Washington in the American Revolution and with both Lee and Grant in the Civil War.

One story that has been passed down to me is a delightful parable of my DNA.

My great grandparents lived in the state of Alabama. They worked hard and built farms and homes and a life for themselves. A family can dream, can't they?

They learned of a farm of similar size that was available for sale on the other side of the Chattahoochee River in Georgia. They knew how difficult their life was. They dreamed that there was a place on the earth where life would be different. Perhaps even easier for them.

It took a while. Letters were written and sent and received. Instead of a sale, terms began to be negotiated for a swap of farms and all they comprised. The deal was struck. My family from Alabama loaded all they would carry on a wagon and began the long trek to Phenix City, which is across the river from Columbus, Georgia.

The family from Georgia began the same loading of their goods, and they, too, began a long journey to Columbus.

One auspicious day, the two families met near the Chattahoochee River and traded the few things needed to complete the swap of farms and goods.

Each family moved to their new farm and began life in what they had dreamed would be the promised land. Life went well for both families.

Until that day when my great grandparents began to realize that they missed the farm they had left. They missed their life in Alabama. They longed for what they had given up over the river for the land and house they now owned in Georgia.

As life would have it, the family who now lived on the farm in Alabama began to experience the same longing for what they had left. They missed their life in Georgia. They dreamed of crossing the river and going home.

The correspondence began. Letters were written and terms were negotiated for a swap of the farms and all they comprised. Both families loaded their goods on their respective wagons. Both families began the long journey to the Chattahoochee River and the bridge between Columbus and Phenix City.

The two families met near the Chattahoochee River and traded the few things needed to complete the swap of farms and goods.

And so, it is proven once again that there's no place like home.

28

JOY DESPITE THE OTHER

> Now may the God of hope fill you with all joy and peace
> as you believe in Him, so that you may overflow with hope
> by the power of the Holy Spirit.
>
> —ROMANS 15:13 (BSB)

Have you ever considered the context of most joy? Joy is seeing and living in God's presence and activity even during difficulty and pain and suffering. Again, joy is seeing and living in God's presence and activity even during difficulty and pain and suffering.

Joy is often not easy to see. It often not easy for joy to live in a culture that insists that joy is a private flood of good feelings.

Is it OK to tell the truth about church? Because there are people, there is always disagreement and adversity in every church, in every congregation, in every part of the Body of Jesus Christ.

There is adversity and disagreement even in those churches that imagine, or pretend, or want you to think they never disagree on anything.

However, the Body of Jesus Christ, the congregation, the church, is to rejoice with one another, to rejoice together, in the Lord. Joy is incomplete unless it is shared. Joy is a sign of the presence of the Risen Christ in our midst.

If a life was shaped and formed through pain, yet joy, how would it look?

If a life was formed through suffering, yet gentleness, how would it sound?

If a life was seasoned through difficulty, yet prayer, how would it taste?

Gary was born in 1959 in Macon, Georgia. His mother managed a household of folks coming and going all the time. His dad was a physician with the Veterans Administration in Dublin, Georgia.

Gary was born with cerebral palsy. In those days, he was called very handicapped. Neither Gary nor any of his family was embarrassed by that term. Gary would never be "normal," but then Patsy Clairmont says that normal is just a setting on a clothes dryer.

Gary was very normal. He was just not perfect at what he could do physically. People whose limitations are on the inside like to pick on people whose limitations are on the outside. Because of assumptions made about Gary's abilities, he was not allowed to attend public school.

Apparently, the faculty thought lack of physical perfection meant a severely damaged ability to be a person in a school.

His parents petitioned and pleaded, but the school board stood firm. No to Gary. So, his dad ran for the school board, but he failed to get elected.

However, Gary's dad had caused so much publicity and so much attention that the school board relented. Gary was admitted to regular classes at a public high school in Macon, Georgia.

He was the first multi-handicapped person ever admitted. Four years later, Gary graduated and made his way across the stage to receive the diploma that he had earned. He graduated in the top 25 percent of his class.

He was admitted to Mercer University.

Four years later, some three thousand people in Macon Coliseum stood and roared with joy as Gary walked across that stage to receive his college diploma—with honors.

His first book was published in 1985. The book was introduced at the Oxford bookstore on Pharr Road in Atlanta at a signing party.

Gary's book is titled, *Everybody is Special: An Autobiography of a Multi-Handicapped Person.*

In his own words, "I cannot do some things as well as other people. So, I try even harder to do the things I can do ..."

A man named Nathan Eddy, from Manchester, England, wrote,

"Joy always takes root amid adversity; there is no other soil for it to grow in."

Gary lived that to be true.

29

IS THIS THE ROCK, OR THE TREE, OR THE EXACT PLACE?

Isn't the cup of blessing that we bless a sharing in the blood of Christ? Isn't the loaf of bread that we break a sharing in the body of Christ?

—1 CORINTHIANS 10:16 (CEB)

There are numerous structures in Israel that have stood for a thousand years ... or more. There are even more ruins of structures in Israel, structures that were destroyed by fire, war, earthquake, or flood.

Pilgrims from the West often ask their guide, "Is this the rock, or the tree, or the place that is mentioned in the Bible?" We did that in 1988 when I was first in the Holy Land. Our guide, Shabtai, listened to our questions about getting precise information concerning locations.

He was gracious. Finally, he said, "I cannot tell you the kind of information you are seeking about these places. What I can tell you is that this is the area of the event in the Bible."

Is that enough? Is it enough to know the area of the biblical event when you cannot get more exact than that? I am satisfied that Shabtai was right with his answer.

I enjoyed messing with him when possible. One day, we were traveling from Jerusalem to the Dead Sea. It was a twenty-five-mile, downhill roller coaster ride with lots of white-knuckle turns. Our bus pulled off the main highway at an exit marked *Good Samaritan Inn*.

We all climbed down the bus steps and gathered at the front of a small,

Crusader-age building of stone. Shabtai began a wonderful monologue about the man traveling from Jerusalem who fell among thieves and was robbed.

Two highly religious men passed by the wounded man because of their laws concerning staying "clean." Eventually, an unpopular man from Samaria stopped and took care of the man.

We were all spellbound. I recalled the story of that man in Luke 15. I also remembered our guide's words about specific places. I raised my hand to get Shabtai's attention. He asked me if I had a question.

I said, "Yes, since this is a parable in Luke and does not necessarily report a specific event, then does it matter whether this is the location or not?"

I never received an answer.

That kind of camaraderie aside, Shabtai took us to one site in Jerusalem that does matter a great deal. That place is also from the Crusader period, so we knew that Jesus and His disciples were never in that building. It is called the Upper Room.

We were in that same room in March 2023.

The Christian season of Lent was underway. The Muslim festival of Ramadan was in full swing. The Jewish celebration of Passover was also being observed. The crowds were expected to be almost beyond management. In some places, they were.

Thus, I had already prepared our group that our visit to the Upper Room would be up a two-story stairwell that would be crowded worse than a Tokyo subway. I also prepared them to expect the small room itself to be crowded from wall to wall. Since I suspected such a crush of humanity was ahead of us, I was trying to allay any fears so our visit might go smoothly.

We arrived at the base of the stairwell, and there was no crowd, nor were there any people on the stairs themselves. We climbed to the Upper Room and were met with an empty room except for a couple seated against the far wall and a single woman taking pictures.

I admit that I was dumbfounded. Thank God, I recovered enough to invite our group to a time of worship. After hymns and prayers, we shared the "Great Thanksgiving" and moved to celebrate the body and blood of Jesus as recorded in that holy event.

As the last of our folks received the elements, I noticed that the couple who were seated across the room had stood and were moving toward me with questioning looks on their faces. I made the universal sign to indicate they were welcome to join us. They smiled and did.

As they were joining our celebration, I also saw the young woman who had been taking pictures was also asking if she was permitted to receive the elements as well. "Of course." I signaled her. She also smiled and did.

That afternoon was wrapped around one of the most profound services of Holy Communion in which I had participated during my forty-nine years of being a pastor.

It turned out that Shabtai was right times two. First, the Upper Room that is recorded in the Bible can be any place where believers gather in Jesus's name. Second, Holy Communion never requires the participants to speak any common language.

Praise God for the rocks and for the trees and especially for the events!

30

SUCH A BILLIE

Honor her for all that her hands have done, and let her works bring her praise at the city gate.

—Proverbs 31:31 (NIV)

Billie is my wife of thirty-five years. We both loved the beach and all things of the ocean. Over the years, we have spent incredible times with the salt air and the saltwater refreshing our very souls. I looked up the "appropriate" gift for the thirty-fifth year of marriage. It is the gift of coral. I know that's right.

Our wedding was at Wesley Chapel United Methodist Church in Marietta, Georgia, on a Saturday night in April. We were married, although she did not think I was going to follow through with the vows. Our friend, Wayne, was officiating. The vow that is repeated as the rings are exchanged is: "With this ring, I thee wed."

I had performed weddings for years. I failed to tell Billie how much I knew. Therefore, I was doing things the "right way" when we came to our vows for our rings to be exchanged. I thought the vow with a ring was one sentence of six words, even though there is a comma after the first three words. Wayne also knew how the vow was to be said. He knew that the vow was two separate phrases of three words each.

He said to me, "David, give Billie her ring and repeat after me: 'With this ring ...'" He paused for me to repeat those three words. I didn't because I was waiting for the other three. I was waiting for: "I thee wed." Wayne paused.

When I didn't speak, Billie thought I was backing out of the marriage.

I stood calm as a cucumber … or some other vegetable. Fortunately, I realized the words as Wayne expected me to give them.

So, I cooperated and spoke the two sets of three words as I gave Billie her ring.

Pain and suffering avoided. *Faux* and *pas* were swept from the room.

After we were married, we celebrated a wedding trip with five children.

These included a friend of my son, John, so he would not have to deal with the younger children. Thus, we began the journey known as "blending a family." You never quite finish that loving task.

Billie and I had begun noticing each other sometime before our first date. As my friend Bruce once said, "She has both outer beauty and inner honey." Yup to that. I also was drawn to her persistence and drivenness.

I was serving on a retreat team, a team to which I was to give a talk of about fifteen minutes. I was speaking positively of a woman and used the word "stubborn" in referring to her. I was taken to task by a member of the team because she insisted, "Women are not stubborn. You must find another way to describe her."

I was fine to do just that. I corrected myself and described the woman as "persistent and driven." Those words were acceptable to the one who was critiquing my talk.

Billie's greatest expression is through her relationship with people she loves. Her first husband had three children from a previous marriage. Those children—Cassie, Ian, and Jenny—came to live with Billie and him shortly after they were married. She later gave birth to her own biological children, Scott and Melanie.

When we married, she accepted my two children as her own. She told my daughter, Lesley, "I may not have carried you in my womb, but I carry you in my heart."

Billie has always been wise beyond her years. She is bright and intelligent. She was and is my helpmeet in ministry. She is honored by family and friends for gracious gifts of love and prayer. She is a superb teacher and an excellent student. She supported and typed and computered me through my doctorate and beyond. She is my best friend.

Earlier in our relationship, we enjoyed time with my parents in Thomaston, Georgia. Dad had retired there but did not ease up on his art and craft of *catching* fish. You may know some who go fishing a lot. My Dad refused that word. If we did not catch our limit or fill the cooler to the brim, we stayed through hail and flood and dark until we did.

He and Mom loved to go to a private lake that was just outside town. The bluegills were on the bed. We picked up crickets and Catawba worms at the bait shop and headed to the lake. I would use the proper spelling, which is Catalpa, but nobody south of anywhere does that. The bream were tearing up anything that came near them.

The best approach to the beds was to step out onto a stone-covered area and cast about twenty feet to the catching place. Billie stepped onto the stones and cast her bait into the lake. I was already in love with her. My mom had accepted her as a competent cook and all-around great woman. My dad was still evaluating, until she hooked a hand-sized bluegill and began the fight. We did not realize she was standing in a fire ant nest the size of a basketball. Catching can do that to you.

Billie was born to dance. She can move her feet to any music at any time. As my parents and I watched, we knew that she was in great pain from the bites of those nasty ants. Despite all the ants could dish out, Billie never stopped reeling her Zebco and landed a trophy bream. Only then did she deal with the ant stings.

My dad beamed and said, "That's a keeper." I knew he meant so much more than a reference to a fish. For thirty-five years, I have constantly thanked God that Billie considered me a "keeper" as well!

Happy thirty-fifth, woman that I love!

31

YOUTH MINISTRY

Let no one despise you for your youth, but set the believers an example in speech, in conduct, in love, in faith, in purity.

—1 TIMOTHY 2:14 (ESV)

What a youth group!

They came from five different high schools to meet every week at Saint Mark Church in downtown Atlanta, Georgia. I was officially appointed as their youth minister, but it often was the other way around.

One of my favorite seasons with them was in the weeks before Christmas. The church offered a living nativity on the front lawn of the sanctuary which edged up to Peachtree Street. I had seen and participated in outdoor nativity settings before, but not like the one offered each year by this group of youth.

An open shed made of pine slabs was set up facing the street. A wooden manger was set in place for baby Jesus. Members of the youth group found bathrobes and dressing gowns and turban-like head gear so that Mary and Joseph, the shepherds, and the wise men all made appearances right in Midtown Atlanta.

A stereo system with large loudspeakers was set for Christmas music to be played. My job was to make sure the music worked and then to stay out of sight. These remarkable youth knew exactly what they were doing.

There was another thing that set the Saint Mark nativity presentation apart from all the others I had seen. Several of the girls had worked diligently at the art of ballet.

They were dressed in white outfits that included large, gossamer wings. As the music played, they would come to life and greet the newborn king with a graceful dance of welcome.

I would stand to the side in the shadows and marvel at the sights. Sometimes, people out for a stroll would stop and watch for a while. Others would be driving past the church and would stop at the curb for a glimpse of this magical offering.

My admiration for these youth was never more profound than the winter it was at and below freezing when they presented their nativity scene and dance. No one would have thought it wrong for them to pack it in and stay warm, but they refused. The intersection of Fifth Street and Peachtree Street came alive on that frigid night with praises to God as my youth group danced for joy!

We also did a retreat at least once a year. That meant we all piled into the church's van and drove to some rustic building that was set up like an army barracks. One year, the van and most of the group made the journey and were looking to unpack and prepare supper.

We made up the salad. We toasted the bread. We found the spaghetti noodles. We had the sauce. We could operate the stove. Our problem came when we realized that we did not have the strainer so we could drain the water out of the noodles. The strainer was in a box in the car of a group member who would not arrive until the next day.

Hmm. We strained our brains for solution. Nothing came to mind.

Finally, I took a clean T-shirt and used it as a filter for the spaghetti. It worked. No one got grossed out. Well, there was that one. We feasted, and shared a time of worship, and later found our way into our luxurious bunk beds. I am still moved in heart by the best thing that group ever did for me.

My best friend was killed in Vietnam. I was serving in the army in Germany and could not get to his funeral and burial in Arlington

Cemetery near Sandy Springs, Georgia. I was carrying what is known as encapsulated grief. I had never seen his grave, nor had I ever really mourned his death.

I was led by God to ask a clergy friend of mine to prepare a memorial service for me at Billy's grave. When I told the youth group about what I was doing, they asked if they could attend and stand with me. I agreed. I cannot adequately describe that afternoon. I cannot tell you all the powerful emotions that flowed around and through us in that Georgia sun. Perhaps in reading this, you might be nudged and encouraged to ask someone to assist you in your grief.

I may omit a name. If so, I regret that my memory is flawed. Nevertheless, God bless you:

Richard
Nancy
Hayes
Jimmy
Libby
Sarah
Lee
Jana
Laura
Warren
Liane
John
Lyle
Cindy

32

A PRODIGAL

God sent a messenger to David's house …
—1 Samuel 19:11 (CEB, Bowen adaptation)

In the summer of my fifteenth year of life, we moved. I was unhappy. I did not know how to express that feeling in healthy ways. I took that pain and hid it behind staying busy. I competed. I pushed myself. I was in turmoil, but not so as you would notice. I appeared almost casual and carefree.

I went from being a straight A student to a terribly average C student. I went from the old and familiar to new town, new house, new school, new church, new people, and new everything in my life.

I began to excel in one thing. I began to excel in anything that kept my emotional and my spiritual pain hidden from sight. I replaced my inside pain with outward physical struggle and suffering. I played through broken ribs, broken fingers, and separated shoulders. I was learning to spell "macho" really well.

After high school graduation, I went to a junior college on full scholarship. But I did not believe that I belonged. I believed I was not enough of anything to be there, and to prove that, I either made an A or a D. After five quarters, I left to return home to my parents' home and to work in a shipping clerk job and to attend college at night.

1966 came with one more step up in Vietnam. I was going to be drafted, so I enlisted with my best friend. We both wanted to find that rush, that thrill, that dangerous edge, including being as close to death as we could get. We were actually looking for love, but in all the wrong places.

We got all we had asked for. Two-and-a-half years later, my friend was dead. I was honorably discharged and back in Atlanta in my parents' home.

I was alive, but I was not really living—Georgia State University at night with the G.I. bill, full-time job in a department store. My parents had moved to the Ben Hill community of Atlanta.

I could not sleep. I was fearful and running between hidden, untreated depression and grinding anxiety about most everything. Some of you know the kind of stuff I was using to find and keep numb.

I was also making sure that I was about as far from God as I could get. I had made my profession of faith and been baptized as a young child, but I had no relationship with God, or Jesus, or the Holy Spirit.

I had bought a 1963 Plymouth Valiant with a six-cylinder engine and enough room inside the hood that I could walk around inside, but it had a fine stereo system and ear-splitting speakers.

On a Saturday summer afternoon, I had almost finished up washing the car at my parents' house—car doors open, radio up to 99.99 percent, so my spirit was about as numb as my body. Hot sun.

I heard the man coming down the cement driveway before I saw him. He was shuffle-walking and dragged a leg as he walked. He was a sharp-dressed man in a three-piece summer suit, tie knotted up well. He carried a large sample case, and as he walked, he also drooled saliva and wiped with a white handkerchief.

I ducked down behind the car, believing in my heart that he would not notice me. I was also believing that he would not see the car, hear the music, or notice the man hiding with the car doors open wide.

He dragged and wiped his way over. He leaned past the hood and yelled over the music, *"Uh wunt du buy dweeting tards?"*

I could still pray. I prayed, *Go away.*

So, as an answer to my prayer, the man leaned down even further and said, "Ah hab nict dweeting tards for dale. Du uw wunt du buy dum?"

I pointed to the house and yelled for him to speak to my mom. He made his way from me to the house and spoke to my mother. Then, up the driveway he shuffled and was finally gone. Almost.

A few minutes later, my mother came to ask if I had met the nice young man who was earning his way in life going from door to door with an assortment of greeting cards and stationery.

It was sometime later that I heard the voice of God asking me to examine my own life. God said, "David, you are trying so hard to punish yourself for so much. I need you, but right now you are not much good to me. I want to heal you. I want to make you whole. I have work for you."

I said, "Oh yeah. What work?"

God said, "I want you to come home. I want you to die to as much of your guilt and shame and self-destruction as you are able right now. I am asking that you accept that you cannot be well and whole without me and my love, and mercy, and grace."

"Then, I will use you to tell other broken and wounded men that they also can become well and whole. It will take you the rest of your life, but I am asking you to start now. I will not push you or force you."

God continued, "That is why I sent such an outwardly broken, and imperfect, and troubling man to you. He is doing well on the inside. You are a mess on the inside while you insist and pretend to be fine.

"Just as you are, I love you. Just as you are, even doubting your very worth, I want you to work with me. Just as you are, join me and get on with your living."

It was in that moment I realized as surely as God provided for, and cared for, and loved that leg-dragging, saliva-wiping, child of His, He also cared for, and loved, and had provided for me.

You can be at home in every way that you want to pretend and still be lost. The grace of God is searching for us. Praise God when we hear and listen!

33

THE LESLEY CABIN

||||||||||||||||||||||||||||||||||||||||||||||||||||||||||||||||||||||||||||||||||||||||||||||||||||||||||||||||||||||||||||||||||||||||||||||||||||||||||

Come to me, all you who are weary and burdened, and I
will give you rest.

—Matthew 11:18 (NIV)

Did you ever go to camp during the summer?

I got to attend Boy Scout camp in the mountains of North Georgia
for eight years in a row. I was blessed with all the challenges that Scouting
could offer a young man in such a wonderful place.

My favorite camp of all was Camp Glisson, a Methodist church camp
located near Dahlonega, Georgia.

I was first there because my father was the preacher for the week and
my mother was camp nurse. I must have been seven or eight years old.

I remember daydreaming about being a teenager so I could participate
in all the things that I was only able to hear or see from a distance.

I got my wish. Being there as a camper was an even better experience
than I had dreamed. I lived for a week in a cramped cabin with other
knuckleheaded boys. I swam in a natural pool that was formed by a
sixty-foot waterfall as it jumped and dove down the rock face of Cane
Creek. I climbed a mountain behind the dining hall to an outdoor chapel
in the woods where a campfire lit the faces of the climbers. I joined my
imperfect voice with a hundred others as we sang on the porch after supper.
I worshiped in a glorious stone chapel whose glassless windows opened to
the trees all around and whose rafters housed at least one barn owl a year.

My mother left me a brass plate that reads: *You're closer to God in a garden than any other place on earth.* That plate sits in our front yard right in front of the knock-out roses.

So, yes, close to God in a garden is right.

Yet, no, because Camp Glisson is a place where drawing closer to God is a constant gift for anyone who has eyes to see, and ears to hear, and a heart open to wonder.

One of my great joys was to be able to invite my own children to spend a week in the summer at Camp Glisson. First John, and then Lesley was drawn to the majesty of that place.

They were as thrilled and excited as I had ever been. Lesley even learned her new favorite song and wanted to teach it to the youth and others at the church I was serving. The song is "Sanctuary." Do you know it?

Then, Lesley died.

She had been at our home earlier in that September week and was reassured that she would be at Glisson come the next summer.

It took a while. Grief can be so powerful that doing anything seems overwhelming, but I knew that I had to do something with my grief or I would fade away.

The idea began to grow that I was to offer some kind of memorial at Camp Glisson in her memory. I knew that musical instruments did not last forever in mountain heat and damp.

I met with Bob Cagle, who was the director of Camp Glisson, to tell him of my wish and see what he might have in mind. Like a new sound system or a piano or something.

He was so energized as he unfolded the dream that was being born for the future of this beloved camp. He outlined a vision of rebuilding every structure on the place into a modern, spacious replica of a North Georgia gold-mining town. They had secured a brilliant architect, and the plans were all set. One thing was lacking: someone was needed to sponsor the rebuilding of the first cabin.

Are you serious? Yes!

Lesley's family and friends all joined in the project. The foundation was laid. The structure began to rise.

The "Lesley Cabin" would not have been possible without the love, and generosity, and sweat of a group of men from the Methodist church in Chamblee, Georgia. I salute you, gentlemen!

Lesley died on September 23, 1995. We dedicated the cabin during Senior High week the next year with a service of worship in the chapel. That was the week that she would have attended.

The cabin is on the left, just up the cement steps from the old dining hall where we ate and sang with our hearts. The plaque on the front door of her cabin reads:

> *This cabin is dedicated by family and friends to celebrate the life of Lesley Ayn Bowen July 3, 1996.*

By the way, we sang "Sanctuary" that day. Do you know that song?

34

LAST YEAR AT THE JORDAN RIVER

||||||||||||||||||||||||||||||||||||||||||||||||||||||||||||||||||||||||||||||||||||||||||||||||||||||||||||||||||||||||||||||||||||||||||||||||||||||||||||

> Peter said to them, "Change your hearts and lives and be
> baptized, each one of you, in the name of Jesus Christ.
> Then God will forgive your sins, and you will receive the
> gift of the Holy Spirit."
> —Acts 2:38 (Easy-to-Read Version)

Please read that verse again. Thank you.

If that is not a major wow for your heart, then maybe you should read it a third time. Baptism is linked in our hearts and lives as a follow-up to change.

Baptism is about the water, but, again, baptism is so much more than the water. For far too long, denominations in the South have been divided over the amount of water that is to be used in the Sacrament of Baptism. I have always sought to offer the place and the day and the amount of water to be celebrated in baptisms based on what the Lord reveals to a person who wants to be baptized.

I have rejoiced with people in their baptisms in sanctuaries, chapels, ponds, swimming pools, metal livestock watering troughs, and streams, as well as on the front steps of a church building.

My favorite baptisms have been those I got to celebrate in the Jordan River during our trips to the Holy Land. It is difficult for me to "stay cool" on the days that I know will end at the Yardenit Baptism Site near Tiberius,

DAVID G. BOWEN

Israel. A section of the River Jordan has been dammed up, so the water does not overwhelm those who are being immersed in the river.

You already know or might have guessed that there is a major gift shop at the site. The good news is that the gift shop also offers the rental of a long, white robe, a towel, and access to a changing room with hot showers.

After folks had changed and prepared themselves, we gathered near the water, where words of Scripture were read and a prayer offered.

Some in our group felt led to answer the leading of God by having Jordan River water poured or placed on their heads from a bowl. I filled a bowl and celebrated with them.

Many in our group wanted to be fully immersed in the water and Spirit, some to remember their baptism and others to be baptized for the first time.

There is a powerful blessing for me when a friend from my congregation joins me in immersing others. I immerse that one first, and then they assist me. I can still see their faces and call their names as I type.

Last year, Jim was immersed and then assisted me. Our son John had joined us in Israel. He wanted to remember his baptism, and my heart still pounds with the power of that moment. I always have someone immerse me, so that I, too, remember my water baptism. I had already met with John and asked him to be that person for me.

He and Jim spoke the ancient words as I was plunged beneath that flood! Could love, and mercy, and grace be more powerful?

I had not seen that a man had approached my wife, Billie, as she photographed us from an overlook.

He was a tour guide who had brought a couple from Nigeria and a couple from the Dominican Republic for a one-day trip from Jerusalem, so that they could remember their baptisms in the Jordan.

He asked if I would celebrate the gifts of water and Spirit with them. I was honored to remain in the water with Jim. The two couples made their way down the steps to the river where we stood. As we moved each of them under the Jordan, we shared the ancient words of Baptism.

Jim and I were so different from these four—languages, nationalities, colors, amounts of hair—yet, a burst of Scripture became more real than ever in my life that day. All the differences melted away.

> There is one body and one Spirit, just as you were called
> to the one hope that belongs to your call, one Lord, one
> faith, one baptism, one God and Father of us all, who is
> above all and through all and in all.
>
> —EPHESIANS 4:4–6 (RSV)

Hallelujah and amen!

35

GENEROSITY AND HALLELUJAH

You will be blessed in every way, and you will be able to keep on being generous. Then many people will thank God when we deliver your gift.

—2 CORINTHIANS 9:11 (CEV)

Her name is Pauline Norton. She died in 1955. She was the older sister of my mother. She was my aunt. She grew up in Athens, Georgia. She worked for the telephone company when there were only operators who asked, "Number please." She never married and spent most of her free time caring for her parents in their home.

One of her wisest decisions was to take part of her salary in company stock. That stock became known as "Aunt Polly's AT&T stock," even though it included more than one telecommunications company.

Polly's nieces and nephews were a source of great joy for her. She made sure that each of us felt that we were the most important member of her family. One of her gifts was the great patience required to put together one- and two hundred-piece and even thousand-piece puzzles. I learned from her that you put the outer edges together first and then you can just slide the rest into place.

Aunt Polly was a gracious and generous treasure in my life.

She tragically died in a fire. Hers was the first funeral that I ever attended.

It was her wish that my mother would receive "Aunt Polly's AT&T

stock" in the event of her death. That stock and the dividends that it paid were my mother's independent money. I called it mom's "walking-around money." That may not be accurate, but I think it is the truth.

Mom never revealed what would happen to her AT&T stock when she died. It was a source of security for her. She was generous with the dividends. It was not always noticed, but she quietly took care of a lot of needs and wants in our family with that stock.

I visited with mom and dad after my daughter, Lesley Ayn, had died. I shared with them the wonderful vision of a renewed Camp Glisson that I had been invited to help bring to reality. Mom generously supported fundraising for the "Lesley Cabin," which continues as a blessing to North Georgia children and youth.

Before Lesley died, I had begun the admissions process for a doctoral program at Wesley Seminary in Washington, D.C. I halted that process for a few months after her death. I strongly believed that the pursuit of this doctorate was to be a part of my healing.

I shared this educational dream with my parents. They began to look at each other as if a great "something" was in the room with us. Mom explained that she had wanted to divide the AT&T stock among the grandchildren at her death. Now, she had decided to do something more immediate. Would I be willing to enter the program at Wesley on a scholarship that would be given to me in Lesley's name?

The weeping took a while.

I managed to say yes and to thank her and Aunt Polly for such generosity.

One of the things that drew me to Wesley for my doctorate was that the seminary held its graduation every four years in the National Cathedral. If my math was correct, I would walk the main aisle of that great building in four years.

Salty grace will find its own way, won't it?

I made the difficult decision to pause my studies to care for a family member that required the attention that only I could give. I was saddened, but I knew this was the right decision for me. My classmates walked that aisle in the National Cathedral in May 2000. I watched it on TV.

Life is also filled with grace and second and even third opportunities, isn't it?

My responsibility to my family changed in 2002. I contacted Wesley and was told that the faculty there was deeply concerned that I would not complete my doctorate. I was instructed to take a few classes and begin the work on my final project.

The months flew past. I finished all the requirements and submitted my work to Wesley. I was accepted for graduation in the National Cathedral in May 2004. Robe and hood secured. Hotel reservations made. Delta airline reservations made.

Mom was able to fly up and share all the celebrations with Billie, my brother, and my sister and her family in Washington. We spent a week of great joy.

The morning of my graduation came. I left my family to gather with other graduates in the cathedral. We processed down that aisle as the great pipe organ thundered in full splendor. My mom sat to the left of the pulpit area. She had secured a wheelchair to facilitate her movements.

A magnificent sermon based on Genesis 26:18–22 was given, and hymns were sung. Finally, the president of Wesley began to call our names. As he did, our families were asked to refrain from applause until all of us had received our hoods.

I was among the first to be called. I heard the president say, "David George Bowen." I moved to the front of the cathedral to shake his hand and to receive my hood.

Despite all the instructions, my mother was not going to resist. As the word "Bowen" faded a bit, she took that silence to shout as loudly as she could, *"Hallelujah!"*

Her word echoed and rang for a moment among the stones of that wonderful place. As it did, I was sure I heard the soft whisper of "Amen" from Polly and Lesley.

DAVID G. BOWEN

36

THAT NIGHT, A LONG TIME AGO

So they hurried off and found Mary and Joseph, and the
baby, who was lying in the manger.

—LUKE 2:16 (NIV)

His name was Sam, and like his name, he was short. His parents had
actually named him Samuel Moses, but like some small children, he did
not like his whole name. He thought about it for a while and announced
that he was Sam.

His family were farmers. They lived out of the country, away from
the noise and the hurry of the town. They grew most of their own food,
although his mother had to shop at the open-air market in town for things
they could not grow. It was a good life, and Sam liked living on that farm.

His father had given him a special job. He was responsible for selling
the hay that was left over after food for the animals on the farm had been
stored. One day, his father had come to him and said, "Sam, you sell that
leftover hay and I will pay you a coin for each bundle you sell."

He liked that idea. It is good to have money in your pocket. The jingle
helps keep away lots of unhappy thoughts. Thoughts like: *I have no money
for a baked treat* or *I have to say no when my friends ask me to go to the fair.*

Sam liked going to town to sell the hay. There were people in the town,
and a good hay-seller always goes to where the people gather.

Sam could sense restlessness in the air. He thought it might be a storm
coming in from the West.

When the wind blew from that direction the animals would become nervous, and Sam could read the animals. But this was not the case. There was no strong wind that day.

He also thought it might be the lack of rain during that fall and winter season. Farmers were always talking about water, and if there would be enough, and what they would do if not, but rain had been plentiful.

When he arrived in town, he found out what was making everyone nervous. The government had added another burden to people by adding a tax to register your birth. The people were not happy, since they already paid some sixty percent of what they made to the government. No wonder there was a lot of noise, and talking, and confusion, which stirred the air around small children like Sam.

Nevertheless, people wanted to buy his hay, and soon he was left with only one bundle. This was actually a bundle of hay that got into his small wagon by mistake. It was the finest hay from the farm, hay that was meant for only the plow horse whose hard work made the farm profitable.

His dad had mistakenly put this bundle into the leftover hay by accident. Worse, no one wanted to pay the extra money that Sam needed to charge for such prize hay.

The long afternoon passed, and Sam was tired. He pulled his wagon with the hay bundle into the back of an abandoned outbuilding that he knew and fell asleep on the soft hay.

He awoke with a start. It was night. He heard the voices of a couple trying to negotiate with the barn owner for a place to sleep for the night. The man was offering them the barn since there was no room for them in any other place in the town.

The barn owner retreated into his own house as the couple began to talk quietly. Overhearing them, Sam was stunned to learn that the woman was pregnant and was soon to give birth to a baby. She would give birth to her baby in that barn where he was still lying.

Sam and his brothers and sister had all been born at home, where they were surrounded by care and comfort. He had an idea. He spoke to the couple and offered the bundle of soft hay for them to place in a feed trough, so the new baby would have a comfortable place to sleep.

They accepted his offer and, pulling his wagon, he rushed from the barn into a remarkably clear night. The sky was such a deep blue that it seemed to have a life of its own. Then, all of a sudden, the sky was split with a great light. Sam thought it must be the full moon of December until he looked back at the barn.

He could make out the faint shape of that building over which was suspended a star so bright that it nearly blinded him. At first, he was a bit frightened for the new baby and that couple, but then, a peace came over him and he began to hear, ever so softly, something like singing.

Sam began to laugh. It had been a good day, and now somebody was singing him home!

37

THE TASTE OF SALT

Salt is good for seasoning.

—MARK 9:50 (NLT)

Does salt have a taste? I know the obvious answer, but what is the taste of salt?

I learned our daughter, Lesley Ayn, had died earlier that day. I was shocked speechless. I was broken up inside. I was brain-numbed.

Once back at our home, I noticed the flood of unexpected tasks that surround a home when someone dies. There will be visits, and questions, and phone calls, and food, and inquiries, and detail upon detail in addition to all the emotions struggling to be expressed.

I did not know where to turn. I was lost. The man who spoke was silenced. The man who did could not. The man who felt was overwhelmed.

My wife, Billie, took a phone call. The call was from a group of women with whom she had been meeting for several years. They were called the Slick Chicks. This group met regularly for fellowship, and support, and accountability. They were calling with a plan that we were to follow.

The plan was simple. A rotation had been outlined. We would not answer the phone. It would be done for us, and records would be kept of who called and the gist of their message for us.

We would not answer the doorbell or the knocks at our door. It would be done for us, and records would be kept of who visited and their expression of condolence.

DAVID G. BOWEN

We would not cook, or clean, or bother with any household tasks. All of that would be done for us. A log would be kept of food that was brought, and food containers would be marked for later return.

We were instructed to take care of anything pertaining to Lesley's funeral. Anything beyond that task was not ours. So, we did.

I did not want to plan that funeral. I did not want to be a grieving parent. I did not want my wife and our other children to suffer such grief.

Toward the end of the Gospel of Matthew, Jesus speaks to those who would listen. He describes the ways in which our care for one another is also caring for Him. Through the tender mercies of a group of women, we experienced just such care.

We were brought to tears at their ministries.

Did you know that tears have a taste?

> If I take the wings of the morning and dwell in the
> uttermost parts of the sea, even there your hand shall
> lead me, and your right hand shall hold me.
>
> —PSALM 139:9–10 (ESV)

I was in high school. A friend invited me to go with him and his family to an Easter Vigil at the Monastery of the Holy Spirit near Conyers, Georgia. The service began at 4:30 a.m. I was deeply moved by everything I saw, and heard, and felt in that lovely sanctuary.

Seven years later, I attended the same service at that early hour. Again, I was stirred by the majesty and the mystery of that place. As a result of those two experiences, I began to set aside time each year for meditation and healing in the retreat house of the monastery.

Many years after that, I was in a muddle. I was serving a wonderful congregation. I could stay as pastor and continue the good work that we had been given, or I could move to a new assignment that I had been offered. I could not decide. I needed guidance. I contacted the monastery in Conyers and reserved a place at the retreat house.

On the way there, I stopped by a feed and seed store and bought a large bag of wild bird feed. I knew there was a large flock of geese that lived on the lake at the monastery. I wanted to spend some time with them, and the feed would make me their welcome guest. I was right. I experienced a calming in my soul as I sat by the lake for several hours.

At dinner that evening, I was approached by a man that I knew. He invited me to a special service of prayer, which was to be held in the crypt later that night. The monks led the service.

One of the readings was Psalm 139. I was blessed and fed by the simplicity of that powerful time.

After the time in the crypt, I made my way to bed and was soon asleep. In my dreams, I was rhythmically moving my arms. My arms became wings, and I was in a V formation as part of a flock of wild geese. The other geese and I shifted positions in our formation as we climbed higher and higher.

I was able to clearly see the land below us. I realized that we were flying directly over the buildings and the parking lot of the church that I was serving. I strained to look. My car was not in its usual spot.

Therefore, I concluded that this was the answer to my "stay or move" dilemma. If my car was gone, so was I.

Over the years since that time with the geese, I have learned a far more profound lesson. The Word from Psalm 139 was not to decide for me. The Word was that God would lead me and hold me on the journey of my life. His great faithfulness would never be determined by me, even if I was at a monastery or I was flying into the dawn with geese.

39

WHEN THE STUDENT IS READY, THE TEACHER WILL APPEAR

So I am eager to preach the good news to you ...
—ROMANS 1:15 (HCSB)

There are at least three things that create awkwardness among colleagues. One of them is cancer. What do you say to a person who is suffering with disease and illness? How do you treat them? I don't say this in public, but I believe there is something innate in us that fears we might catch the disease.

The other two are the death of a child and divorce. Even among ministers, there are the same fears about these two as there are about cancer.

The death of Lesley was devastating. The valley of the shadow has revealed the presence of the One who loves us most and who grieves with us. Still, it is a place of the long shadows.

I have shared with you several stories about Les and her place in my life, even in her death. So, I leave her for now to tell you another.

My divorce was costly. There is some shadow that remains over divorced people. I am not bitter. I hold no grudge or wish for payback.

Yet, I knew that my presence was sometimes discomforting to others, even other clergy. I avoided several gatherings and meetings because I was ill at ease with myself. I made sure I would have other plans when the time for pastors' school came around. We can be silly, can't we?

I missed my friends. I missed corporate worship with them. I missed the preaching and teaching from the giants of our calling to ministry.

I heard that Fred Craddock would be the keynote preacher at the upcoming pastors' school at Saint Simons Island on the coast of Georgia.

I wanted to attend. I made my reservation.

I also carried some reservations as I traveled from my home to this event.

Fred offered a series of sermons on the great images in the Book of the Revelation at the end of the New Testament. He invited us to the New Jerusalem. He showed us the Four Horsemen. He reviewed Satan Expelled from Heaven. He carried us into the presence of the Throne and the Lamb.

Each sermon was more powerful than the previous. Fred's words and illustrations were clear to our minds and hearts. We prayed and sang the love of God. I was filled to the brim with grace and mercy. Best of all, I was touched by a hope for which I had longed. I wept my way through each of Fred's sermons. I attempted to keep those tears to myself, but there were some who loved me enough to notice.

He finished the last of his sermons on the last day of that pastors' school. The crowd around him was appropriately large and noisy. I waited until the space around him emptied. I extended my hand and said to him, "Sometimes you wonder why you chose topics for sermons. These were for me personally."

It was then I realized he had never let go of my hand. He also kept looking into my heart. He never said a word. He did not have to.

You see, he had preached the Good News!

40

IT'S IN THE BOOK

> If a fellow believer hurts you, go and tell him—work it out
> between the two of you. If he listens, you've made a friend.
> —MATTHEW 18:15 (THE MESSAGE)

I could not figure what I had done to have this person dislike me so. I am far from perfect. That means I can be responsible for something that is interfering with a relationship and never know the reason.

My divorce caused me and my children great pain. That divorce, though unwanted by me, also caused some other people in my congregation some pain as well.

One woman reasoned that if God had called me to the ministry, then God would have provided me with a true "preacher's wife." In some ways, I thought she might be right.

She had some other negative things to say about me, but I never knew how to deal with them. Something unwell was festering between us.

One Sunday I was given Matthew 18:15–17 as the text for my sermon. Have you ever read those words? They are strong.

During my preparation for that sermon, it was revealed to me that God did not want me to just preach on that text. I agonized over that text because it was so simple and so straightforward.

There is not a lot of wiggle room in that Word from God's Word. I sought the counsel of my prayer warrior and my mentor in all things spiritual. I did not like that she referred me to this same passage from Matthew and left it with me.

I asked my disciple Bible study class to meet me at the altar of the church and had them pray for me and the situation.

They had no details of what I was doing. I simply asked them to cover me in prayer.

I had previously called this woman and asked her to meet me at a place of her choosing.

She chose her home with her husband in the next room with the door between the rooms to be kept open.

I arrived. After some small talk, I asked her if I could read the passage from Matthew 18. She agreed and we began.

I said to her, "For several years, you have tried to hurt me professionally. You have tried to run me off from this church, and in all ways you have sought to discredit me. Why? What did I do to you?"

She said, "Nothing. You never did anything to me."

"What? What? Then why?" I asked.

She said, "Do you remember your first winter here as our preacher? You were to go rabbit hunting with my husband and another member of my family."

That had been years earlier, and I honestly could not remember, but I said yes anyway.

She said, "You did not go."

I said, "You are right. I remember now that a huge snowstorm started Thursday afternoon, and it was to be blowing bad all weekend."

I continued, "Since I preach twice on Sunday morning, teach Sunday school, and then preach on Sunday evening, I did not need to be out in a swamp all day Saturday and get sick. I called your husband and the other family member on Thursday afternoon and said I could not go."

She said, "Yeah, and for that reason, that member of my family has never set foot in church again."

I was stunned.

I was moved to ask her forgiveness for anything I had done to her or to anyone in her family. She graciously accepted. Then, she offered me forgiveness and asked for reconciliation between us.

We talked for a long time, sharing tears as well.

She and I experienced Matthew 18:15–17 as if the words had been written just for the two of us.

They were.

41

JEB AND KYLE

The Lord looks down in love, bending over heaven's balcony.

—PSALM 53:2A (THE PASSION TRANSLATION)

Balconies are important in lots of places.

Where would Romeo and Juliet be without that impassioned conversation about location, location, location?

Where would John Wilkes Booth have had access to assassinate Abraham Lincoln?

Where would crabby and cranky Statler and Waldorf sit to throw insults in the Muppet Theater?

The Methodist church in Hogansville, Georgia, had a small balcony that overlooked the sanctuary and, particularly, the pulpit area.

During my first year as the pastor, I had never climbed the tight, winding staircase that led from the foyer of the church building up to the three rows of seats in that balcony.

Jeb and Kyle sat there in the first row every Sunday.

I knew these two to be real characters. They were not destructive troublemakers. Yet, one of them usually wore a grin to indicate something was afoot and they were likely the cause.

I had the privilege of working with them on a Boy Scout award called "God and Country," and we had become friends.

One thing I began to notice about Jeb and Kyle: when I was preaching, they sat in that balcony with eyes focused on me like laser beams. I watched to see if they nodded off asleep. Not once.

Or if they got bored and yawned like most adults. Never.

It got to be too much for me. One Sunday in my second year, I waited until the congregation had cleared the sanctuary. I made my way up the stairs to the balcony. It was there I found the secret to their attentiveness.

There, spread out between where the two of them had been sitting were the bright-inked comic pages of the Sunday newspaper.

They took turns watching me. One would read and be entertained while the other kept lookout in case I looked up at the balcony while preaching.

If I shifted my eyes toward these two, a hand-signal would alert the reader to join the watcher in rapt attention to my very words.

I never ratted them out. I think that would have been an insult to their creativity. We just kept their secret in the balcony.

42

COMING HOME

|||||||||||||||||||||||||||||||||||||||||||||||||||||||||||||||||||||||||||||||||||||||||||||||||||||||||||||||||||||||||||||||||||||||||||||||||||||||||||

> My people will live in safety, quietly at home. They will
> be at rest.
>
> —ISAIAH 32:18 (NLT)

Twenty years is a long time. That much time had passed since I joined the US Army. I was not alone in that July 1966 surge of men and women entering active duty. We were young. We were enthusiastic. We were so naive about what really lay ahead for us. We were all to be deeply touched by Vietnam.

Few of us have ever really known what to do with that experience between 1959 and 1975. The lives of some will forever be seared and burned by what they saw and did there. Others will always set an extra place at their heart's table for someone who will never come home again.

My best friend was killed in Vietnam on March 6, 1969, but in a way, I never came home either. I have felt inexplicable guilt and shame that he was killed, and I, working in an army hospital in Germany, was not.

There is a wall in Washington, D.C., that contains the names of those who died in Vietnam. I had not been able to see it, because I knew the cold black stone held the name of Billy Gene Creech. I didn't know if I could face the reality that the name is buried somewhere other than in my heart.

As I entered the park and stared at the wall, I must have looked as lost as I felt. A volunteer, retired from whatever she used to do, asked, "Can I help you find a name?"

She gave me more than half an hour of her time as we found name after name blasted into that stone. She gave me a crayon and paper so that I could make rubbings to take back home to the families who had asked me to find a name for them.

But her real contribution was in her wisdom.

I had brought a poem that I wrote in 1976 on the tenth anniversary of my military duty. I was going to leave it at the base of panel 30W, which contains the name of my best friend from high school.

My nose was running. My eyes were spilling all over my face. I couldn't fully cry, so I was making a strange noise. The lady spoke very gently. "The best thing you can do for him is to remember. The best thing you can do for yourself is to cry." So, I did.

One hour is not an eternity. Noon until 1:00 p.m. was the time I had set aside to sit on the grass opposite my friend's name and to remember him. As my watch neared fifty-nine minutes, a shadow came over me. I looked up into the faces of a man, his wife, and three children.

Speaking in low whisper, he asked, "Can you help me? I'm new here, and I wanna find my buddy's name."

At the sixtieth minute of my hour, I was walking with him to find the name of a friend killed in 1971. As I left this family, I spoke to my brother-in-arms. "The best thing you can do for him is remember. The best thing you can do for yourself is to cry." I handed him what was left of my Kleenex.

I moved up the walk and away from the memorial, I met a third person who taught me about remembering. Hers is a special age. Not yet five years old. I could tell because she unceasingly questioned her father about everything she saw. He did a remarkable job with his answers, considering the enormity of the task. One part of their conversation continues to touch me deeply.

"Dad, whose names are these on this wall?"

DAVID G. BOWEN

"Hon, these are the names of the Americans killed or missing in a far- away place called Vietnam."

"Dad, where are the names of all the people who were not killed in Vietnam?"

The father paused for a moment. He then said, "Hon, those would be our names."

It struck me that it was all right not to die in a rice field in Vietnam, that's OK to come home.

I gave the wall the gift of my poem that day, and the wall gave me a gift in return. I was told it's OK to do some things with my life that I want to do, that I don't have to hide anything anymore.

The Vietnam memorial is not a temple. Not everyone's politics will allow them to visit there and to leave with a sense of peace.

I swear, on that day, I was standing on holy ground.

David G. Bowen

RA 14936769

43

HOW LONG FOR A HABIT TO FORM?

Have I not given you your orders? Take heart and be strong; have no fear and do not be troubled; for the Lord your God is with you wherever you go …
—Joshua 1:9 (Bible in Basic English)

Raise your hand if you ever ate at the Majestic Grill on Ponce de Leon Avenue in Atlanta.

OK, at least some of you know the place.

I ate there only once in my life. It was a rainy July day, but the burger and fries at the lunch counter made it a bit brighter.

But not for long.

It was the day I was inducted into the US Army, and things went somewhat sideways after my last meal as a civilian.

From the Majestic, I walked down to the old Ford assembly plant where I was greeted by lots of olive-drabbed people who wanted me to quit being me and become an "us."

I joined lines for things like the shortest physical exam on record. Then, some shots. Then, some questions.

The "us" were then taken into a large room where we were invited to each raise our right hand and to take an oath. I swore to support and to defend the Constitution of the United States and to obey orders.

Next came the first of more than 16,591 instances of "wait here" until we were told what to do.

Please believe that being told what to do was readily available for the next few days.

Some thirty-six of us were invited to take a packet of papers and to find a seat on an olive-drab bus whose odometer read *critical care required*.

If you have ever taken a flight on an old-school Martin 404 airplane, then you know much of what that ride was like.

How long did it take you to drive from Atlanta to Columbus, Georgia? On purpose?

We left when it was one day. We arrived at a reception center at Fort Benning, Georgia, later the same week.

The bus door was jerked open, and a wide-brimmed brown hat that covered the loudest pair of lungs in human history greeted us in our seats.

The lungs were speaking through a very tall mouth. That mouth cordially informed that none of our mothers would be present during the next several months of our lives.

We were further informed that our bodies were no longer our property, but they, in fact, had now been given over to an uncle of ours.

Finally, we were invited to assume a position that was to become familiar. It is called the "low crawl." I had done some casual low crawling in my previous life, but never on a bus so that I could crawl off said bus and onto the sidewalk that awaited us.

Georgia pavement has never been kind to human skin, particularly on the knees, but the hatted voice encouraged us to keep crawling all the way down the sidewalk and into an olive-drab building.

Several of the guys in our crawl formation had trouble with this procedure. Their complaints were lovingly received and noted for the record.

Fortunately, I was not first in line, so the door to the building was already shoved open by the faces of those who led our procession.

We slowed to a slower crawl. Another voice appeared from above us.

That voice was wearing olive drab with two stripes on its sleeves. You may know better, but I reckoned those stripes had taken nearly twenty-three years to be earned by the wearer. You could tell this by the kindly way he invited us to stand, one at a time, and reach for a plate that was shoved onto a metal tray.

Next came a suggestion that we secure matching silverware, take a beverage from the table, find a seat, and keep our faces shut.

We did exactly that.

It was then I looked down to see what had been so gracefully deposited on the plate in front of me.

It had originally been a bright-green, and probably very happy, bell pepper, but several days of assault and battery had reduced it to a mere shell of its original self.

Worse, the green shell had been filled with rice that had become a messy paste. The rice was mixed into and through a brownish meat whose origin is still lost in the mists of time.

Let the record show that I was not alone in halting my fork above the pepper thing.

It was then the voice under the hat came alive as if it had been waiting for us to pause.

The instructions were as clear as Jack Nicholson reminding Tom Cruise about his intent to give a direct order.

"Eat the green treat or I will help you eat it."

"Us" all did just as we had been instructed.

To this day, I can raise my right hand and take an oath that such a broken and sorrowful thing as that stuffed bell pepper delight has never again come close to my lips.

There are friends who insist that my aversion to stuffed, green, globular things can be overcome with the result that I might even like them. In support of their helpful attitude, I quote from a Google website, personaldevelopmentwisdom.com:

"It **takes** about **21 days to form** a new **habit**. … According to Phillippa Lally; a health psychology researcher at University College London, a new **habit** usually **takes** a little more than 2 months — 66 **days** to be exact — and as much as 254 **days** until it's fully **formed**."

Wrong! It only took me one evening.

44

IN CELEBRATION OF BEING WRONG

Do not fail to show love to strangers, for by doing this some have welcomed angels without realizing it.

—Hebrews 13:2 (EHV)

I did not grow up in a family where your car was a measure of who you were and how important you were to the people around you. Cars were transportation. They were useful for getting you from place to place in a timely fashion.

But a pair of roller skates were a different matter. The best was those worn at the roller rink and no place else. Mine were wheels on a piece of metal that was clamped to the bottom of my shoes. A large, metal key turned the clamps. I never had a pair of shoes whose soles were rigid enough to make the clamps effective. I spent most of my roller-days stumbling about as my shoes came loose from the clamps.

I did better with the greatest gift to early-teen mobility in the small town where we lived. It was a bicycle. In my late twenties, I could afford a bright-yellow, ten-speed beast with a derailleur instead of a chair that ate my pant legs.

According to Wikipedia, a derailleur is "a variable-ratio bicycle gearing system consisting of a chain, multiple sprockets of different sizes, and a mechanism to move the chain from one sprocket to another."

Until that French-inspired purchase, I sat atop a generic-brand turtle with wide tires and no mechanical advantage of any kind. When our gang

DAVID G. BOWEN

rode bikes, I always trailed the bunch to make sure we were never going to be ambushed from the rear.

One of our gathering spots from which we would organize rides into the streets of our town was a tennis court that a guy had built beside his house. It was several years before I picked up tennis, but it was a good place to meet up and plan for the day.

Three houses down the street and away from the tennis court was that house. *The Man* lived there, or so the rumors had it. I only knew that he was to be feared. We only saw him though the single slat of a Venetian blind that was finger-lifted as he spied on the street.

Maybe he was a "mass" something or other. Maybe he was so disfigured that he was permanently housebound to save the neighborhood children from nightmares. I never knew all the rumors, nor did I cease to wonder what terrors lurked inside that house.

One rainy afternoon, I was racing at tortoise speed from the tennis court to my home when a car swerved too close to the side of the road where I was furiously pedaling. Because of the ditch, I could not move any further off the pavement. I would have been fine except my left foot came off the pedal of my bike and planted itself into the spokes of my front wheel.

Rolling a tumble or two, I lay on the edge of the road and watched the car drive away. I was hurt. I knew I had injuries. My foot was still lodged in the spokes, making it impossible for me to move or to get up.

Not a single other car came or went down that street as I lay there. I heard footsteps before I saw anyone. I spotted a pair of large bedroom slippers as I moved my eyes from the ground to see who had walked up. It was him. It was the guy in the house. It was *the Man* everybody feared. He was the one about whom nobody knew anything for sure.

He was nowhere as big or as evil-looking as the rumors.

I think I was crying. No, I am pretty sure I was.

He asked, "Are you badly injured?"

I said, "No."

He said, "You are the Bowens' kid, aren't you?"

"Yes," I replied.

He said, "I called them. They are on the way here right now. I think you are going to be OK. Can I do anything else for you?"

"No, thank you," I said as I checked for his wings to sprout.

DAVID G. BOWEN

Let us think of ways to motivate one another to acts of
love and good works. And let us not neglect our meeting
together, as some people do, but encourage one another,
especially now that the day of his return is drawing near.
—Hebrews 10:24–25 (NLT)

They called themselves the "Inklings." They were students at Oxford
University during the 1930s. They were literary enthusiasts who gathered
to discuss literature and to exchange stories they had written. C. S. Lewis
and J. R. R. Tolkien were the more famous members of the group. *A
Hobbit, a Wardrobe, and a Great War* by Joseph Loconte offers an excellent
account of how World War I changed the lives of these young men.

We were not students at Oxford. We were theology students at the
Candler School of Theology of Emory University, near Atlanta, Georgia.

We were all serving local Methodist congregations while we completed
our graduate degrees at Candler.

Can you imagine that a small office supply shop, and a neighborhood
hardware store, and a Waffle House were all melded into one building?

It was called Horton's, and it was located down the hill from the main
administrative offices of Emory.

There were never many of us who met at Horton's for breakfast on a
regular basis. The grill area had seating in booths. The cook was named

Charles. He was the best short-order grill man I ever saw. He never wrote down any orders but stirred wonderful breakfasts for us.

There were probably more sophisticated names for our group. I have given us the name "Theologs" since I am the one telling this story. During those far too brief years, we sat huddled around plates of food for our bodies and engaged in conversations to support and to encourage one another in our ministry.

Upon reflection, there is no way that anyone could simultaneously attend graduate school, serve a local congregation, and be present as a member of a growing family. Yet, we did, and honestly, we did all of that quite well.

I don't recall that we ever set forth any guidelines or parameters for our meetings at Horton's. We met to share our faith as Christian pastors and to support each other in the very hard work of loving others in the church.

In the years since Horton's, I have had the privilege of meeting with women and men who were just starting the journey of becoming ordained ministers and pastors. My assigned task was to encourage and support the group with stories of my joys and my challenges in ministry.

Sitting at this computer, I realize I was suggesting that each of these candidates for ministry find a place that served good food for their bodies and invited loving encouragement for each other around the table.

No matter what their meeting places were called, I know that they all looked a lot like Horton's.

46
RATS IN THE SWAMP

||||||||||||||||||||||||||||||||||||||||||||||||||||||||||||||||||||||||||||||||||||||||||||||||||||||||||||||||||||||||||||||||||||||||

[H]e who looks at the earth and it trembles ...
—Psalm 104:32 (NIV)

My phone rang. It was my friend Lee. He wanted to know if I would like to be a "Swamp Rat." I hesitated a bit. I had been in lots of swamps in my life, but never as a rat.

He explained that the group was made up of all sorts of guys who loved to canoe. Their major trip was to travel to the Okefenokee Swamp in Southeast Georgia, where they would spend five days and nights on the Red Trail. The put-in point was Kingfisher Landing, and the take-out was Stephen Foster State Park.

I got all excited since I had canoed in the Okefenokee for years as a Boy Scout.

I said, "Sure, count me in."

Lee said, "But ... but we are doing the swamp in the spring. For now, we are going down the Little Satilla River for about thirty miles. It'll still be good."

That river makes its serpentine journey through pine forests. It is about fifty feet wide and has wide sand beaches all the way to the Atlantic Ocean.

We assembled our gear and food for the trip. We met at a rally point to load eight canoes onto a trailer that was pulled behind a van. Since I was the newest Swamp Rat, I was given the privilege of riding in the back of the van among all the bags of gear for the trip.

Lee sat in the passenger seat. Our driver asked if we minded stopping near Lumber City, Georgia, to drop off a package for a friend of his.

"No problem," we said.

As it turned out, there was a problem. Our driver had no idea how to find the house of the man for whom the package was intended. Lumber City is a wonderful town in the middle of vast pine forests. Sections of the forest are connected by dirt roads that criss and cross for more than a hundred miles in any direction.

We crissed and we crossed for several hours, but we never found the right house. As we were about to give up, we spotted the rooster tail of dirt that another vehicle was throwing up as it went along. We headed down another road to intersect this truck. Our driver lowered his window as the driver of the truck did the same. The two drivers spoke the same words at the same time: "We are lost. Can you help us?"

They exchanged their shared ignorance of the area. However, we were finally able to get enough information to locate the house that had been lost for half the day.

Now, we were on our way.

For almost a week, rain had been falling and collecting all along the area of the Satilla River. Our fearless leaders told us that the raging flood water would not be a problem. We would adjust our schedule so that we would spend fewer days on the water.

We pulled the van into an unloading zone and stowed our gear in the canoes. Lee took the stern seat while I was paddling in the bow.

Within ten minutes of paddling, we realized that I was much too large for that arrangement.

We switched places for me to sit in the back and steer while Lee provided the muscle up front. Our seat-swap was not easy. We had to pull to shore. That meant we would be the next-to-last canoe out of the eight that were headed south.

Finally, we were set for the Little Satilla.

DAVID G. BOWEN

Well, not quite. The deluge had changed the slowly meandering river into a mile-wide sweep of a river. Instead of occasionally paddling, we were going to steer and guide our canoe to avoid overturning in the rapidly moving water.

We were moving so fast that we zoomed past the spots where we were to spend the first two nights. Finally, our leaders pulled into an area where we could camp. Lee and I unloaded our gear and set up for the night.

Then, we all stopped to listen.

We could hear faint cries for help from up the river toward where we had left the van. It was then that an overturned canoe came into view. There were several bundles and packs also moving toward us in the general area of the canoe. It was obvious our guys had tipped over and were in real trouble.

Lee and I volunteered to take this empty canoe and pull it behind ours to rescue our fellow Rats. We underestimated the current. We struggled for almost two hours to reach the area of the two canoeists.

They had managed to reach a small grove of pine trees that was about seventy feet from a bend in the river. They had climbed onto the lower branches from where they were clinging and yelling at us.

We paddled past them and came back with the current to shove their canoe under the trees.

It was then that the blade of my paddle hit solid ground. Our two buddies were desperately seeking safety in trees that were standing in less than three feet of water. They looked like drowned rats.

Our trip down the Little Satilla took less than three days. We loaded all the soaking gear and went home.

The next spring, I finally got to canoe with the Swamp Rats in the Okefenokee. Lee and I were canoe partners again. I was now a veteran, so I did not have to ride in the back of the van with all the gear. We had a new guy join us, and he got the honor of that position.

On the trip from Atlanta to Waycross, Georgia, he revealed that he had two gifts. One was complaining about anything and everything. He did that very well. Complaining is a universal right, and so we supported him until we had enough. However, he would not ease up on just how bad his life had become.

His second gift was playing practical jokes on all the guys. Again, enough can get to be enough in a hurry, but he would neither cease nor desist.

The Red Trail in the Okefenokee begins with water-filled grasslands and winds its way to a wooden platform for the first night's stay at a place called Gator Lake. There is a scattering of small cypress trees that surround the platform on two sides. The lake is named for the hundreds of alligators that thrive in the water.

After sunset, we placed headlamps on the top of our heads and cast the light out onto the water. Immediately, the light revealed pairs of red eyes as far as we could see.

Our complaining and joking specialist kept up his irritating routine until he finally fell asleep. I admit nothing. I am just stating the facts as I remember them. To those who have never been in the swamp, it seems there would be no wildlife that would be able to reach a wooden platform in the middle of a gator-infested lake. They would be wrong.

Raccoons love to travel in trees to reach food that is carelessly left out by canoers and campers. Raccoons also love Fritos. The legend is that a trail of those corn chips began from the edge of the platform near the trees. That trail led to the sleeping bag of the whining joker and ended in a pile just inside the bag.

I am pleased to report that no serious wounds or lasting scars resulted from the quiet arrival of a family of raccoons into the down-filled slumber of our newest Rat. Some label what happened that night as behavior modification. We called it "welcome."

47

SIDE EFFECTS OF A MISSION TRIP

||||||||||||||||||||||||||||||||||||||||||||||||||||||||||||||||||||||||||||||||||||||||||||||||||||||||||||||||||||||||||||||||||||||||

Declare his glory among the nations, his marvelous deeds among all peoples.

—1 Chronicles 16:24 (NIV)

Did you ever pretend when you were a small child?

I used to pretend I was a missionary in some foreign county. I would line up stuffed animals, and dolls, and even another child so I could talk and teach and preach to them. I have no idea what I said or even if I said anything worthwhile. The content of my words did not seem to matter.

Then, one day, it happened. I had been serving local congregations for some fifteen years when the invitation came. Two other pastors were forming a mission team to the island of Grenada. They would be joined by a large group of laity to rebuild a church structure that had been damaged in a hurricane. The team would also lead worship and visit the people of the island.

Was I interested? I leaped to be included. The plans were set for our trip. We would gather at a local church parking lot for prayer and assignments for the trip to Grenada. I joined the lay folks from our congregation as we anxiously waited for the others to arrive. The team leader was hesitant to start our meeting. I thought that there must be a bad traffic situation that was delaying the arrival of our companions.

Finally, the team leader shared that the other two pastors would not be joining us. He also told us that there would not be any other laity to fill out the team we had thought would be rebuilding the damaged sanctuary.

Then, he dropped the third shoe. Instead of flying to Miami and then on to Grenada, we would be riding in a church van from Marietta, Georgia, to Miami.

I was certain that I had lost my hearing, but his bad news was true.

We would have only one third of the team needed for construction. Instead of three pastors to preach and lead visitation, I would be responsible for all those ministries.

There may have been a bit of tension in that van on the incredible long drive to Miami. Thanks to the leadership of the Holy Spirit, we were led to prayerfully resolve the bubbling conflict.

We arrived in Miami and spent the night sat a missionary facility. We boarded the flight to Grenada and lifted off in a British West Indies Airline (BWIA) jet. In the hold of the plane was our luggage and the three sections of a prefabricated steeple, which would be assembled on the site of the damaged sanctuary.

I had never flown on a "local" flight in the Caribbean. That word meant we stopped at four or five of the other islands before we settled down on the tarmac in Grenada. We were met with all kinds of bureaucratic delays until a stranger stepped in to explain our situation to the authorities. It seemed that all the construction tools in our luggage had added to the confusion that the parts of the steeple had caused.

Finally, we were driven to our quarters to unpack and enjoy dinner. It was at that meal that I was told I would be preaching the next morning in the church building that we would be rebuilding. The journey to that site would mean I had to rise, shave, shower, get dressed and be ready at 6:00 a.m. to travel.

Fortunately, the van driver would become a dear friend, so the frustrations I was carrying were diffused by the time we arrived at our destination. There were about a dozen people in worship that morning.

Yet, it was a powerful time for me as I talked about the glories of God and the deeds of Jesus as recorded in the New Testament.

There was also a goat that wandered in and out of the building during our time in worship. The door to the building had long since been blown away, so the goat was always welcome. I did not realize that it was a sign of a later encounter.

After worship, the van driver and I made our way back to join the rest of the team for lunch. It was at that meal that I was told I would be leading the visitation during the afternoon. Honestly, my tank was empty. I was spent. Still, I had waited all my life for this mission opportunity, so I swallowed my weary spirit and asked God to provide what I needed.

He did.

I was assigned to visit a family who lived up the side of a hill and somewhat away from the town. I walked toward their house when I realized they lived in a makeshift dwelling with pine slabs for walls and a tin roof. The floor inside was dirt.

I was welcomed with great enthusiasm. This family had been waiting for months to entertain the American pastor who would be spending the afternoon with them. Their hospitality was strong as we sat and talked about our faith in Jesus. They told me that I would be their guest for the evening meal, and they hoped we would share Holy Communion before I left.

I was honored. I also noticed that the lone chicken I had seen running round their home had disappeared. The meal that evening would be that chicken, the only protein they would have for a few days.

My tears would not stop.

Following that evening with my new friends in Christ, I was carried on spiritual wings back to our residence. Our team was awakened the next morning to a wonderful breakfast and to begin preparations for the trip to the church house.

We arrived to find that the prefab windows for the sanctuary had been damaged in shipment. Putting that task aside, we began work on the massive front door and the new pews. The wood we were to use quickly dulled all our saw blades.

At least the sections of the steeple had safely arrived. As we stood and contemplated our dismal circumstance, we were greeted by a hello from across the street. Our neighbor wanted to know if we needed any help with our project. Let that rest with you for a moment.

The man was a retired master carpenter. He had a metal cabinet filled with the tools that were required for our projects. He also had access to glass panes so that our prefab windows could be healed. The day that had begun in such darkness had been revealed to contain the miraculous grace of God in human form.

Two days later, I was asked to lead a funeral service for a woman whose pastor was out of town. I said I would be honored. For many years, I had led funeral services. This one was so powerful. The sanctuary in the Methodist church was filled with song, and prayer, and testimony for the life of the beloved saint.

I met the funeral director as we exited the building. He told me that we would be walking behind the hearse as we made our way to the cemetery. The hearse was a huge Ford station wagon with the tailgate raised for the coffin to be fitted inside. Two large speakers were then installed at the end of the coffin so that our walk to the cemetery was accompanied by the sounds of Country Charlie Pride singing gospel tunes.

At the cemetery, the pallbearers were stopped because the grave had been cut as a rectangle, while the coffin had two sides that extended out. The funeral director handed me a shovel so I could join him in the grave to cut out the sides of the grave to accommodate the coffin. As we dug, I heard a familiar noise above my head. It was a herd of goats that lived in the cemetery and kept the grass trimmed off the graves.

Our team was able to complete all the work that had been planned for us. On our final day, we formed a human pyramid so the sections of the steeple could be lifted to the roof and bolted in place. After that task was done, we gathered with the congregation for the closing time of worship.

We packed our luggage and were driven to the airport the next morning for the flight to Miami. Our BWIA pilot had heard of our remarkable mission journey to his country. As a salute to the glory of God and to the deeds done in Jesus's name, he tilted the plane so that we had a broadside view of the church house before we straightened up for the flight home.

On that last leg of our journey, I prayed that I would never recover from that time in Grenada! God is faithful, isn't He?

48

ONLY WITH LONG HAIR ... AND SHE SINGS

Say to wisdom, "You are my sister," and to insight, "You are my relative."

—Proverbs 7:4 (NIV)

Her name is Judy. She is my relative. She is my sister. She has both wisdom and insight. She makes up puns and laughs at them. She is an accomplished vocalist. She sings solos in her church in Virginia. She also sings in the choir and takes part in drama presentations.

I have had the privilege of traveling to many places in the world with her. In 1968, we saw Germany when I was stationed there in the army and Judy was in the traveling company of Up With People. With our spouses, we have delighted at weeks together in Alaska, Israel, and Ireland.

One of my favorite occasions was at a dinner in Ireland. Our group was seated around a long table. My wife, Billie, wanted to take the mandatory group photo. Judy and I were seated next to each other at the table. We were looking across at another friend when Billie yelled, "Turn your heads for the photo." Of course, she meant to turn our heads and look in her direction.

Without a pause, Judy and I both turned our heads so that our backs were to the camera. I don't recall that many people at the table laughed like the two of us.

Judy also does a talk with the children on Sunday mornings in her sanctuary. She calls these "Small Talk." The following is a talk that she recently offered:

Forty years ago, on a hot summer day in Hinesville, Georgia, I was driving down the road when a very elderly black woman stepped in front of my car. I stopped immediately. I was afraid I would hit her.

But again, she walked in front of my car. Finally, I rolled down my window and said, "Can I help you ma'am?"

She said, "Child, I see the love of Jesus on your face!"

I was stunned and speechless. No one had ever said anything like that to me. After a moment, she said, "Child, I need a ride."

I said, "Yes ma'am. Let me get the door for you."

I went around the car to open the passenger door. She got in and buckled up. She needed to go to a health clinic. The facility was a few miles down the road. It was way too far and way too hot a day for her to walk that far with her cane. So, off we went. I was still amazed that she saw the face of Jesus on me. What did she see on my face that caused her to say that to me?

We all have Christ inside of us, but how do we let him shine through us so that people see him on our face? The answer that Christ gave is found in Philippians, chapter 2, verse 7. In the Revised Standard Version, that verse reads: "[He] emptied himself, taking the form of a servant …" I like to use the word helper in place of servant, because we must help others when we are in pain, hurting physical or emotional mental pain. The way to empty ourselves is to help others look for a way through prayer or the scripture for guidance and forget about ourselves. Through this process, self becomes less important, and Christ comes more visible through the love of God.

Hmm. Judy is my sister. I love her. She is one of the few people who would call that kind of wisdom and insight "Small Talk." Like so many good storytellers, she spoke her words toward the children that day. Yet, her words found our hearts and lives as well.

49

THE BACK ROAD NEAR LAKE WEST POINT

I was a stranger and you invited me in …

—MATTHEW 25:35 (NIV)

The Chattahoochee River flows from the mountains of North Georgia and empties into the Apalachicola Bay south of Panama City, Florida. On the way, the river waters the city of Atlanta and provides recreation opportunities in the names of Lake Lanier and Lake West Point. Lake Lanier is located northeast of Atlanta while West Point is situated on the border of Georgia and Alabama.

I was serving as pastor of a Methodist congregation whose members lived in and near Hogansville, Georgia. The closest hospital and major shopping centers for my people were in Lagrange, Georgia. The quickest route to LaGrange is Interstate 85. When possible, I like to take the back roads that wind through the countryside and past Lake West Point.

The day was blowing early spring. It was rainy with a strong wind that chilled anyone out on the damp. I had been visiting a member of my congregation who was in the hospital in LaGrange. I was headed home and looking forward to the warmth of food and an evening with my family.

I saw the man ahead of me. He was walking on the side of the road with his head down and his thumb out in the universal sign of "I need a ride." I pulled my car to the side of the road, rolled the passenger window down, and waited for him to walk up to the car. Looking out from under a soaked hat, he bent to look in the window.

I grinned and said, "I'm going to Hogansville if you need a ride."

Without speaking, he opened the car door and slid into the passenger seat. After buckling his seat belt, he extended his hand and spoke two words.

"Ben Worthy" was what he said.

What I heard was, "Have you *been worthy* of the Lord's blessings that you have received all of your life?"

I was speechless. My brain was flooded with all the things that a person given to pretending perfection in his life can imagine.

If I made a 99 on a test or an exam, the voice in my head asked if I could have made a 100 with more preparation.

I never sat up straight enough in public. I rolled up throw rugs and small carpets as I walked over or near them. My elbows had a mind of their own and were always finding their way into a table where they did not belong.

I am not always plagued by these kinds of self-doubts, but they do visit from time to time. The good news is that the love and forgiveness of Jesus does not depend on my perfection or on my lack of it. Can I get an "amen"?

I realized that my passenger's hand was still extended toward me and that I had not spoken in return.

"Ben Worthy," he said again.

"David Bowen," I replied and shook his hand.

Ben became a fixture in my life during the years that I spent in Hogansville.

That afternoon on the back road near Lake West Point was some fifty years ago. I often think of Ben and that day. When I do, I get to laugh at myself, and I stick out my tongue at perfection.

50

TASTY GRACE

||||||||||||||||||||||||||||||||||||||||||||||||||||||||||||||||||||||||||||||||||||||||||||||||||||||||||||||||||||||||||||||||||||||||||||||||||||||||||||||||||||||

*They also brought ... honey and curds, sheep, and cheese
from cows' milk for David and his people to eat.*

—1 Samuel 17:28 (NIV)

Every congregation that I served had some kind of ministry with and to
older adults—XZY Club, Saints Alive, Golden Agers. No matter the name
of the group or organization, the formula was always great food and as
much "age-appropriate" fun as we could endure.

So it was with that group in Cobb County, Georgia.

I counted myself a member and was graciously welcomed by the leader
of the pack, one Sarah Ann. There are some expressions in the Southern
part of the United States that just fit a person. She was a "mess."

She treated each member of our older adult group as a member of her
family. Even Ruth. Ruth had been born with a serious deficiency. She could
not make any type of dessert, even if she tried and precisely followed the
recipe. It was a running source of amusement for Sarah Ann and me, but
we never revealed it to anyone else.

For years, Sarah Ann had managed to avoid having Ruth sign up to
bring anything to our monthly gatherings that resembled dessert. So far,
she had been successful.

Until that one day. Ruth did everything but demand that she would
bring a cake, and cookies, and a pie to the next meeting. Sarah Ann and
I met? What could we do?

We decided that I would contact Ruth and get as much detail as possible from her about all three desserts that she would be bringing.

I succeeded in collecting loads of information like the size, and the shape, and the color, and even the ingredients of her proposed sweet offerings.

The morning of our meeting, Sarah Ann went to work and recreated in her own kitchen those desserts in minute detail. She brought them to the fellowship hall of our church, and we hid them in a janitor's closet.

Ruth arrived with her pie, and cookies, and cake ready to be served and eaten. I met her at the door and made a big fuss over taking them from her and moving them into the kitchen for slicing and serving later in the meal.

The meeting went well. There was wonderful conversation, and friendship, and food for everyone. Then, the announcement was made to move to the desserts.

At the very last second, I had sneaked out the back door with Ruth's dessert offerings and eased them into a plastic bag and then into the garbage can.

Meanwhile, Sarah Ann had placed out for consumption her own version of those same desserts. They were taken, and eaten, and enjoyed by all.

Ruth was as pleased as punch with the way her desserts had disappeared. She was even more pleased with all the congratulations and bragging about them.

Sarah Ann and I stood by and invented an eyeball version of pinkie swear.

51

NOT YET

||||||||||||||||||||||||||||||||||||||||||||||||||||||||||||||||||||||||||||||||||||||||||||||||||||||||||||||||||||||||||||||||||||||||||||||||||||||||||||||||||||||

O God, you have taught me from my youth, and up to now I have proclaimed your wonderful deeds.

—Psalm 71:17 (LEB)

I am in the fourth quarter of my life. I might make it to overtime, but that is not for me to say. I have been incredibly blessed by great teachers and wonderful resources for ministry. With your permission, I want to leave this last story as some recommendations for you, both laity and clergy.

I wrote a sermon that was titled, "Arrogant Humility." What I offer below will be just that.

You need to read some excellent sermons. You need to read them, not so you can preach them, but so you can learn to preach. Fred Craddock and Barbara Brown Taylor are among my favorites. I still open John Claypool's volume on living with pain and suffering.

You need a Bible commentary. The internet will place dozens at your fingertips. I recommend "Feasting on the Word." The set is twelve volumes based on the Common Lectionary plus volumes on each Gospel.

You need to travel to the Holy Land. You ought to go first to Israel by yourself so you can be a pilgrim and soak in all that will find you there. If you go with famous or powerful people, you will miss a great deal. If you go as a group leader, you will never be immersed in the land and the people. Take a notebook and keep a nightly journal. Modern technology makes it possible to have other means of note-keeping, but I like the written word.

You need to be taught a good Bible study so you can be a good Bible study teacher. I delighted to take disciple Bible study training, and then I was blessed to lead groups using that material for some thirty years.

Among the best teachers I know are Ray Vander Laan and Lois Tverberg. Lois offers two books on following Jesus that are superb. Ray has filmed sixteen DVDs in the Holy Land. Each DVD has an accompanying book. I found the books to be more than most people would manage. I reduced each of Ray's lessons to three pages. If you ask me, I will forward my notes on this material to you.

You need to watch great films. *To Kill a Mockingbird* still blesses. *Places in the Heart* has much to offer about forgiveness and Holy Communion. *Tender Mercies* offers so much about peace and grace.

You need to chew some poetry. It will make you more of the wordsmith that all those who teach and preach ought to be. The two volumes by Ann Weems that have Bethlehem and Jerusalem in the titles are strong candidates. Wendell Berry offers life from the farm as well as life deepened by grace. Luci Shaw has opened the grace of God's creation to several generations of seekers.

You need to read some works by fellow disciples of Jesus. Max Lucado's earliest books would make a start. Ken Gire is unknown to most, but he has such a gift for images. Brennan Manning is an honest storyteller who will invite you to examine your own dark places. Denise Hopkins wrote *Journey Through the Psalms* as a unique look at this ancient hymnbook.

Well, that is enough for now. My dad said that a congregation's favorite words were "finally" or "in conclusion." I offer my favorite ending: "Always peace and grace!"

Printed in the United States
by Baker & Taylor Publisher Services